Empowering
People

THE SUNDAY TIMES

Empowering People

SECOND EDITION

Jane Smith

◬ KOGAN PAGE | *CREATING SUCCESS*

First published in 1996
Second edition 2000

Kogan Page Limited
120 Pentonville Road
London N1 9JN

British Library Cataloguing in Publication Data

A CIP record for this book is available from the British Library.

ISBN 0 7494 3391 4

Typeset by Jean Cussons Typesetting, Diss, Norfolk
Printed and bound in Great Britain by Clays Ltd, St Ives plc

contents

introduction

Achieving success amidst the constant demands and the uncertainties of today's world often seems like a massive task. And it's one that no one can hope to carry through without the full cooperation and enthusiasm of staff at all levels of the organisation. The philosophy of empowerment recognises that nobody knows a job better than the person doing it, and that most people want to be involved and take a pride in their work. It all sounds good in theory, but history is littered with well-intentioned but unsuccessful attempts to empower people.

Empowerment is an extremely effective tool for developing both people and organisations – and it is not used widely enough because people frequently see it as an 'all or nothing' option. This book sets out to make empowerment achievable by breaking the concept down into its component parts.

It is my hope that this book will be used to help train and develop those managers 'at the sharp end' who have to cope with changing structures and new approaches. It can be used as a workbook for individuals who are studying on their own; or as a textbook to prepare people for a training course on empowerment. Many of the activities in the text can be used as a basis for discussion in pairs or small groups.

the need for empowerment

Empowerment is a vital element of the modern business environment. Getting closer to the customer, improving service delivery, continuous innovation, increased productivity, gaining the competitive edge – none of these things is possible unless organisations find new ways to empower their people.

Although we may believe that empowerment will benefit organisations, what will individuals get out of it? What does empowerment actually mean? And what can managers do, in practical terms, to empower the people they work with?

what is empowerment?

Empowering people means encouraging them to become more involved in the decisions and activities that affect their jobs. It means providing them with the opportunity to show that they can come up with good ideas and that they have the skills to put these ideas into practice.

'There was a problem because we were not getting a good mpg out of our vans. We tried to work out why this was – bad driving, going too fast, heavy use of the clutch and gears – a combination of all these things probably. So we got the drivers together and discussed the problem, the devastating effect this would have on our budget if the situation continued. They came up with the idea of putting the average 'good' mpg for each type of van on a wallboard and then each month noting down what we were actually getting out of our vehicles. Things improved very quickly after that.'

First line manager in a distribution company

The concept of empowerment ranges:

- ■ from simply encouraging people to play a more active role in their work,
- ■ through involving them in taking responsibility for improving the way that things are done,
- ■ to enabling them to make more and bigger decisions without having to refer to someone more senior.

'It used to be that I couldn't buy a new pen without getting permission from the purchasing manager. Now I have my own budget of several thousand pounds a year. I know it's my responsibility to make it work, and it's certainly not easy. But it does make sense because I am in the best position to judge where the money needs to be spent – and where it is wasted.'

Production manager

In your organisation you will probably have groups or individuals who have become empowered to different degrees. Some may not want to get involved at all, other than carrying out the tasks that they have been allocated; some may become more active for short periods and then opt out again. For others, however, empowerment opens up a whole new way of life. These are the people and teams who want to accept a responsibility that goes beyond their immediate jobs and contribute to making the whole organisation work better. They are active in solving problems and cooperate easily with other individuals and groups.

If you want to empower people, your task is to find ways of moving as many of them as possible from a position where they 'do what they are told and ask no questions' to one in which they will work with you to take on more responsibility.

commitment from the top

But empowerment is first and foremost about changing the role and behaviour of management. It is a process that can only begin in a climate in which there are high expectations, where everyone feels respected and valued and where people will offer their best at all times. It cuts right through the traditional relationship between managers and their subordinates. So here's a 'health warning' before you read any further! Top management must be right behind the move to empower people – without this support you will find the necessary cultural change difficult, if not impossible.

If you don't have support from above, there are a number of options you could try:

■ Put some of the ideas suggested in this book into practice and monitor the results. If you have some success, you can start to make a case for making more widespread use of this approach.

■ Talk to your colleagues about the benefits of empowerment and, with them, put together a presentation for the senior management team. Include case studies that illustrate how other companies have used empowerment to their advantage.

■ Give your boss this book to read and then discuss how you can use some of the processes and techniques in your department.

By doing these things, you are empowering yourself; an important first step on the road to empowering other people.

why is empowerment necessary?

Whichever way you look at it, empowerment is not a passing fad; it is here to stay. And its importance is going to grow because it is fundamental to the developments that are taking place in business today. It goes hand in hand with social changes, with what technology enables us to do and with the demands of the competitive environment.

Ultimately there are two reasons why it is necessary to transform the way that we work with the people in business organisations:

1. The external environment has changed.
2. People themselves have changed.

the business environment

Business organisations in the first decade of the 21st century operate in a world of uncertainty, complexity and unpredictable change. You are probably well aware of the main factors that have brought this situation about:

▓ **Intensifying competition**
All businesses are to a greater or lesser extent influenced and affected by the competitive environment. In the 1980s and 1990s, most UK organisations viewed the home market as the area within which they would do battle. The situation in the new century, however, is totally different; national boundaries no longer form the barrier to trade that they once did. Now competition from overseas represents a substantial threat, while many businesses set their sights on exploiting opportunities in the global market.
Organisations need empowered people to help them fight off the competitive threat.

▓ **Rapid technological innovation**
Any business that wishes to survive in a changing world must keep abreast of the technology applicable to its products and services and to its methods of operation. To do otherwise is to risk destruction as competitors take advantage of new developments. Most companies now use computer systems to help them gather, process, store and use information more efficiently. Many also use them as the basis of entirely new manufacturing processes or services. Sophisticated business information systems have improved general efficiency and have frequently resulted in substantial cost savings. Add to this the new business possibilities offered by the World Wide Web and you have a picture of a business environment that has changed radically in a few short years.
Organisations need empowered people to make the best use of advanced technology.

▓ **Constant demand for higher quality and better value**
Many organisations recognise that, in the face of increasing competition, they have to continuously improve the quality of service they provide for customers. This means finding out what customers want in the first place and then improving on this. When several companies are competing in the same market for the business of the same customers, service is often the most important way of gaining the competitive edge.
Organisations need empowered people to find innovative ways of improving their products and services.

▓ **Growing ecological problems**
Businesses do not have a natural propensity to look after the environment. But organisations that choose to ignore their consumers' political and environmental concerns now run the risk of placing the very future of their businesses in jeopardy. To succeed, businesses

have to try to anticipate consumer reaction to a whole range of issues.

Recent years have witnessed the emergence of green consumerism as the business response to growing environmental awareness. Doing business in an increasingly 'green' world means:

- designing safer, healthier and less polluting products and packages;
- developing less polluting manufacturing facilities
- minimising hazardous waste;
- conserving non-renewable natural resources.

Organisations need empowered people to help them to implement these kinds of policies.

Succeeding in this world means recognising and managing changes before they take control of us. It means developing our organisations in such a way that they will be able to turn the threat of change into an opportunity for growth. But the task is impossible unless we make sure that our people are fully involved in the process of change. To ensure that their goals are achieved, organisations need the intelligence, commitment and energy of the entire workforce.

working people

For a long time managers have been saying that people are their most valuable resource, but until recently few seem to have acted on this assertion. At last it is dawning on organisations that their present security and future success depend more on the talent and wit of their people than on their land, their buildings, their plant and their equipment. Employees have truly become the 'intellectual capital' of the organisation.

In his book *The Empty Raincoat* (1995) Charles Handy notes that 'Focused intelligence, the ability to acquire and apply knowledge and know-how, is the new source of wealth'.

The traditional sources of wealth – land, raw materials, technology, even unskilled labour – can all be bought in as and when they are needed. What you can't do without is the people who have the ability to use all of these to the best advantage. Material resources cannot by themselves improve service quality, they cannot generate innovative ideas, they cannot push the organisation to new performance levels. The goal of empowerment is to harness the brains of our people, rather than simply their brawn.

Another aspect of change is that working people today are very different from those in employment in the middle years of the twentieth century. Traditional 'blue collar' workers now form a minority of the workforce, most workers do jobs that demand far more of them than simple manual labour, and those that are involved in unskilled work have higher expectations than their predecessors.

In addition, it has become more and more common for employees to own shares in the business in which they work. Those that do have an extra stake have a further incentive to take responsibility for the organisation's overall performance.

Among the important psychological changes that have occurred is the greater awareness people now have of their right to fulfil themselves as individuals. They have dreams and aspirations that go far beyond the modest expectations of their parents and grandparents. They are less likely to defer automatically to authority or unquestioningly to accept discipline. Instead, they need to be motivated by tangible rewards or gratification. Working people today have, in general, become less receptive to the idea of 'top down command flow'. The consequences of ignoring their demands and their expectations can be severe for businesses. It would be wrong, however, to view these new attitudes as a problem – on the contrary the people who hold them are a valuable resource waiting to be harnessed.

the benefits of empowering people

This exercise will help you to become more aware of what happens to people when they become actively involved. Think of a time when *you* took on responsibility for achieving something – either on your own or with others.

In the spaces below describe:

▧ **What you did**
(You may have been organising a youth club swimming gala, starting up a residents' association or building your own house. Or you may have been part of a project team at work.)

_____

_____

_____

_____

▧ **How you felt**
(Did you feel confident or elated at what you achieved? Were you surprised to discover some hidden talents?)

_____

_____

_____

_____

▧ **The benefits of your involvement**
(These may have been personal benefits or they may have brought benefits for a small group of people, the whole community or the entire organisation.)

_____

_____

_____

_____

The incident you described may have been a very modest achievement or a major accomplishment that affected large numbers of people. The benefits for you may have included:

- ■ an intense sense of belonging to a group;
- ■ a sense of satisfaction at taking responsibility for achieving a task;
- ■ a feeling that you were doing something worthwhile;
- ■ pleasure gained from communicating and cooperating with other people;
- ■ enhanced confidence from doing something you never believed possible.

The important point is that when empowerment occurs at work, everyone benefits:

- ■ *the organisation* – because individual talents are harnessed to the full;
- ■ *the department or team* – because it becomes more enthusiastic, active and successful;
- ■ *individuals* – because they are stretched beyond what they previously thought they could achieve.

what's in it for you?

We have seen what empowerment offers employees – enhanced job satisfaction, cooperating more closely with others, working with a clear purpose and gaining a sense of achievement when goals are achieved. All these aspects help to satisfy very basic human needs. But what are the benefits for the managers who have to work hard to make these things happen?

To answer this question it is useful to analyse the purpose of the management role, and to match this against what managers actually spend most of their time doing.

1. What is the basic purpose of your job?

    _____

    _____

    _____

    _____

2. What percentage of your time do you spend doing work which is directly relevant to this central purpose?

    _____

    _____

    _____

    _____

3. What percentage do you spend doing tasks that you see as 'urgent', but are not directly relevant to your role?

    _____

    _____

    _____

    _____

Most managers tend to spend far too much time tied up in routine jobs or coping with problems and crises, when what they should be doing are the planning and developmental tasks that are crucial to the organisation's long-term success. The effects of this situation are threefold:

1. *Managers are experiencing immense stress.* It is not unusual to find managers working upwards of 50 hours a week to cope with the tasks of managing existing operations. On top of that they have to deal with constant changes in manufacturing processes, service delivery, distribution and administration systems. And they do all of this in the context of diminishing resources, ever increasing competition and greater demands for better value for money or higher profits.

2. *Managers are wasting their potential.* If they spend their time firefighting, managers are doing nothing to develop themselves or to plan the long-term development of the organisation. Strategic thinking, product and service development, managing innovation, analysing the 'environmental' changes that threaten the organisation or provide it with new opportunities: these are the tasks that managers at all levels should be involving themselves in.

3. *Organisations are under-performing.* Even if agreed targets are met (and at what cost to the health and well-being of the people who achieve them?) it is almost certain that higher productivity or greater profitability could be accomplished by managers empowering their people and freeing themselves to take on a different role.

If *you* are able to liberate yourself from the idea that your job is to direct and control others, you can start to focus on a different set of issues:

- ■ long-term planning;
- ■ encouraging and developing people;
- ■ providing back-up services and support for others;
- ■ generating innovative ideas;
- ■ managing relations with customers;

▓ managing integration with other teams and departments;
▓ involving yourself in special projects;
▓ developing your own skills and knowledge.

By making this transition, you will reap immense rewards:

▓ *Job satisfaction.* You will gain a heightened sense of purpose and take a pride in your achievements.
▓ *Recognition.* Colleagues and the people who work for you will see you in a new light and respect you more.
▓ *Acquisition of new understanding and skills.* The process of empowering others will give you an opportunity to see things differently, to reflect on what you see and to develop new skills.
▓ *Career advancement.* Making a greater contribution to your organisation's long-term success is likely to increase your promotion prospects.

However, there are still some managers who remain determinedly sceptical about the positive benefits of empowerment. As a useful way of clarifying your own ideas, how would you respond to some of the common objections listed below?

1. Empowerment means that a manager abdicates his or her responsibilities.

_____

_____

_____

_____

2. Empowerment equals anarchy!

_____

_____

_____

_____

3. If I empower others, I will be doing myself out of a job.

_____

_____

_____

the barriers to empowerment

Organisations often fail to improve because managers, who have the authority to make changes, are unaware of the problems, while people on the front line, who know what the problems are, have no authority to do anything about them. It is all too common for businesses to pay consultants thousands of pounds to tell them how to improve work processes, when their staff could have provided much of the same information for nothing!

The traditional way of managing has emphasised the control and direction of people and the maintenance of discipline. The old-style manager clings firmly to the belief that 'if you give them an inch they will take a mile'. Such managers have a profound effect on the way their people behave. Rather than focusing on improving services or getting closer to the customer's needs, their subordinates' primary objectives tend to be pleasing the boss and keeping out of trouble.

To empower others, managers have to trust their people's abilities and commitment. To commit themselves and to take on ownership of the organisation's goals, people must be able to trust and respect their managers. And before any of this can happen, managers have to believe that empowerment is both possible and beneficial.

The following excuses have been stifling empowerment for years. Which ones have you heard other people make? (And, be honest, which ones do you make yourself?)

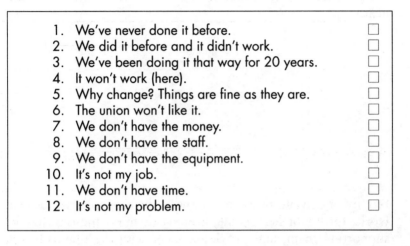

1. We've never done it before. ☐
2. We did it before and it didn't work. ☐
3. We've been doing it that way for 20 years. ☐
4. It won't work (here). ☐
5. Why change? Things are fine as they are. ☐
6. The union won't like it. ☐
7. We don't have the money. ☐
8. We don't have the staff. ☐
9. We don't have the equipment. ☐
10. It's not my job. ☐
11. We don't have time. ☐
12. It's not my problem. ☐

your role

Many managers are concerned that to empower is to lose control and to invite chaos. But you have no need to worry if you recognise that your central task is far more valuable than merely giving orders and punishing failure; your true role is that of a leader.

But a post-millennium business leader should not be a 'Lone Ranger' figure who rides into town and saves the citizens who are being threatened by a bunch of outlaws. What happens if another gang of bandits appear after the hero or heroine has ridden off into the sunset? Clearly it is a better idea to show people how to defend themselves, rather than make them dependent. In this sense the leader is a teacher and an enabler, allowing others to develop their skills by setting their own targets and solving their own problems.

This model of leadership turns the conventional organisational hierarchy on its head. In old-style structures the manager is at the top of the pyramid with all the subordinates underneath.

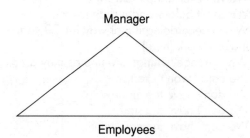

But in organisations that empower their people, the leader works for his or her people, keeping them on the right track, supporting them, and providing them with the opportunities and resources to contribute to the long-term success of the organisation.

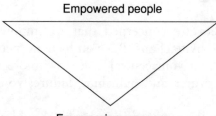

In this new leadership model, the leader is not considered to have his or her 'followers'; the leader of an empowered team is a leader of leaders.

leadership skills

To fulfil this role successfully, managers must possess certain skills and qualities. Although some people are lucky enough to be born with the required characteristics, good natural leaders tend to be an extremely rare breed. Most people have to work hard to learn, practise and perfect the skills of leadership. But this is not to say that all leaders should strive to achieve exactly the same methods and approaches. Being yourself and making the most of your own strengths and individual character is an important aspect of good leadership.

The checklist which follows summarises many of the qualities of good leaders which are highlighted in this book. Use it to help you identify where your strengths lie and plan how to develop the areas where you are less effective. Give yourself a score of between 1 and 4 for each item, where 1 is excellent and 4 is poor.

Do you:	Your score
strive to give people a positive sense of purpose?	1___2___3___4
get the best out of individuals by building on their strengths?	1___2___3___4
act from a belief that others are willing to take on responsibility?	1___2___3___4
create an atmosphere that encourages maximum involvement?	1___2___3___4
feel confident enough to delegate important jobs?	1___2___3___4
provide support for others as required and when requested?	1___2___3___4
demonstrate a positive and sincere attitude towards others?	1___2___3___4
recognise achievements and reward staff appropriately?	1___2___3___4
communicate and listen effectively?	1___2___3___4

make people feel important and valued?   1___2___3___4
understand the values of the organisation?   1___2___3___4
get others to share these values?   1___2___3___4
lead by example?   1___2___3___4

Now make a note of your leadership strengths:

_____

_____

_____

_____

And note down the areas you still have to work on:

_____

_____

_____

_____

Effective leaders are able to empower people because they are confident, self-disciplined and highly motivated. They are not put off by minor problems or even major setbacks, and are willing to take risks themselves and to allow others to do so. Good leaders know that they cannot carry the whole enterprise, the whole department or even the whole section on their shoulders alone, but that the only way to succeed is with and through other people. This is how the organiser of a community arts festival described her role (without, I suspect, even knowing that she was a leader):

'I realised that it was not humanly possible for me to do everything myself. The festival was not going to succeed unless I could get a lot of other people involved and make them want it to happen as much as I did. I knew that my role was to generate enthusiasm, to inspire everyone else with my idea of what it could be like. I had to keep encouraging them too when we came up against major obstacles. This was especially hard when I felt also downhearted at times.'

Jenny, organiser of a community arts festival

providing a vision

Jenny's experience illustrates another of the most important roles of a leader – that of providing a vision. If leaders are to persuade others to go in a certain direction, they must have a clear idea themselves of where that direction lies. The vision that they provide for their people should relate to:

- the overall purpose and vision of the organisation as a whole;
- the objectives and targets of their department or team;
- their own priorities.

A leader's ability to provide a vision for a group of people will influence their commitment to attaining its targets and, ultimately, the quality of their performance. This is because the purpose of a vision is to create challenge, excitement and a common direction for activities.

Without the vision of John F Kennedy in 1961, the United States would never have succeeded in putting men on the Moon in 1969:

'I believe that this nation should commit itself to landing a man on the Moon and returning him safely to Earth before this decade is out... No single space project will be more impressive to mankind or more important to the long range exploration of space... but in a very real sense it will not be one man going to the Moon... it will be an entire nation.'

Visions are important because a leader has to mobilise people around a future that it not yet known. With a vision he or she helps people to attain what seems unattainable. Here is Jenny again:

'Back in January we could only dream of reaching a situation where the village would be buzzing with music, art shows, street entertainment and choirs. We talked about the long July days, being out in the open air and people working together like never before to make it happen.'

Psychologists tell us that it is easier to do things, particularly complex and challenging things, if we first of all try to see a picture of what it is we are trying to achieve. This is called visualising, and it is what good leaders do for the people they work with.

Visions can exist at any level:

■ **A vision for racial equality**
I have a dream that one day this nation will rise up and live out the meaning of its creed. We hold these truths to be self evident – that all men are created equal. I have a dream.

Martin Luther King

■ **A vision for an organisation**
We believe our first responsibility is to doctors, nurses and patients.

Johnson & Johnson

■ **A vision for a department**
We shall become the most efficient part of the whole organisation. We shall achieve our targets, respond to all customer enquiries within 24 hours, feed information promptly through to sales and marketing and strive continuously to improve the service we provide.

Customer Services Manager

There is a story that a traveller once came across three stone-masons who were hard at work. He asked each one in turn what he was doing. The first answered, 'I am cementing stones together'. The second one answered, 'I am making a wall'. And the third one said, 'I am building a cathedral'!

Try visualising what you would like your department or team to become, and make notes below.

_____

_____

_____

_____

How will you communicate your vision to others?

_____

_____

_____

_____

where do you go to from here?

This book is designed to help you develop many of the skills and qualities we have introduced in this chapter. You can tackle the following in any order, depending on which areas you feel should take priority:

- ▨ *Chapter 2*, which deals with creating the right kind of relationships within an environment in which people will feel empowered.
- ▨ *Chapter 3*, which looks at communications skills: getting and giving information.
- ▨ *Chapter 4*, which explores the skills of developing others.
- ▨ *Chapter 5*, which incorporates feedback skills, reward and recognition; using positive influences to empower others.
- ▨ *Chapter 6*, which helps you to plan a programme of practical steps that you can put into operation immediately.

back to basics

Just as you can't grow strong trees in poor soil, you can't empower people in an environment that will not sustain the qualities you want to encourage. This chapter is about the environment in which you grow your empowered people – with the emphasis on the contribution you can make by influencing the culture, by creating appropriate relationships and building empowering relationships.

the culture of your workplace

Usually the word 'culture' is associated with the traditions and the ways of behaving that you find in different countries. It's not just the language – it's people's gestures, the way they eat, the way they behave, the way they relate to each other. These things often seem so unfamiliar when you go abroad – it's all a matter of culture.

In recent years people have begun to realise that organisations, too, have their own cultures. Businesses have their own different ways of doing things, different types of personality that tend to do well, different kinds of relationships that are encouraged. Organisational cultures are shaped by the type of work people do, what has happened in the past and by the kinds of people who work there. Divisions, sections or teams also tend to have their own unique cultural pattern. These local cultures both influence and are influenced by the culture of the larger organisation.

clues about culture

Once you know what to look for, it becomes a simple task to identify the extent to which the culture you work in will help you to empower people.

In Table 2.1, the left-hand column lists some of the characteristics of an organisation in which empowering people is likely to be an uphill battle. The right-hand column, on the other hand, describes an ideal situation – a truly empowering organisational culture. Try marking where you think your organisation, or your part of the organisation, is on a continuum between these two extremes.

Table 2.1   *An empowering culture*

From:	Your organisation or team	To:
The customer is a necessary evil	_____	The customer is king
Employees live with fear of failure	_____	Employees are confident about taking risks
New ideas are regarded with suspicion	_____	All ideas are valued and given consideration
Criticism is expressed freely	_____	Praise is freely given

Table 2.1 *(cont'd)*

From:	Your organisation or team	To:
Problems are seen as signs of failure	_____	Problems are viewed as opportunities for development
Important decisions are made in secret	_____	Everyone is involved in important decisions
Access to information is limited	_____	Everyone has access to information
Managers think they know everything about the organisation	_____	Managers accept that employees may know more than them
People are afraid of change	_____	People have learnt to see change as a challenge
There are barriers between management and team members	_____	Managers have effective working relationships with their teams
There are barriers between different departments and teams	_____	Different departments and teams work well together

The areas in which your marks are nearer the left-hand side than the right will give you some clues as to where changes may be needed in your organisation, or the part of it for which you are responsible. Indeed there may be room for improvement even if all your marks are close to the right-hand side. Empowering cultures never stand still; people who work in them are always on the look out for better ways of doing things.

changing culture by redefining values

Some organisations owe their success to making deliberate choices about the culture they want to encourage. They have done this, in part, by defining the values that they want the workforce to adopt.

The mobile phone company Mercury One 2 One, for example, has adopted a set of values that it believes are associated with advanced business performance.

These values are:

▨ **Empowerment and support for high expectations.** We look for people who expect the best from themselves and we, in turn, expect the best from them.

▨ **People as individuals.** The business of Mercury One 2 One is all about people and their relationship in business, family and social life. Whether it is customer, supplier or a colleague, we always respect people and treat them as we would wish to be treated.

▨ **Families and communities.** We believe that supporting the growth and importance of family and community relationships is important to our business, important to our people and important in a broader social context.

▨ **Straightforward and better.** All changes to our business must abide by the motto 'keep it simple' and be an improvement to our efficiency and cost base to meet all customer expectations and needs.

▨ **Ambassadors for communication.** Communication between people is the lifeblood of our business, so as a business, communication should be one of the things we are best at.

Properly chosen values can help create an empowering atmosphere. Because everyone knows how they are expected to behave, managers can get out of the way and let them get on with it. Values also provide a clear focus for team or individual performance and help everyone to set priorities for their work.

In the space below, suggest some values that you would like your team or department to adopt. Ideally, these will be based on the values that have been defined by the wider organisation. If this is not possible, however, discuss some values with the people you would like to share them.

_____

_____

_____

_____

Once you have identified some values that you would like to encourage your team or department to adopt, make them real by starting to talk about them and by living them. Remember that it works both ways:

■ the values and culture of the organisation affect how people behave;
■ how people behave affects the culture.

your beliefs about people

Our values and beliefs about human beings affect the extent to which we feel able to trust people and to delegate responsibility. For example, how far will this manager be able to let go?

'I can't trust anyone to do anything around here. If you want something done, do it yourself – that's my motto.'

And is this one going to encourage greater personal responsibility among members of his team?

'These people aren't interested in getting a good job done – all they want is the pay cheque at the end of the month.'

Table 2.2 will help you to think about your attitudes towards the people you lead. On each side you will see some contrasting opinions about work and people's attitudes to work. Consider each pair of extremes and then mark the number on the scale which most accurately reflects your own point of view.

Table 2.2 *Staff attitudes to work*

X					Y
People are paid not to think	1	2	3	4	People are intelligent, curious and responsible
People are lacking in creative ideas	1	2	3	4	Many people are capable of creating good ideas
People work solely for money	1	2	3	4	People look for job satisfaction as well as money
People are all the same	1	2	3	4	People are individuals
Managers manage, team members work	1	2	3	4	Managers and team members are both trying to achieve good results
People shun responsibility for their work	1	2	3	4	People like to take responsibility for what they do
Discipline and control get the best results	1	2	3	4	People respond best when given freedom of action
Punishments gets results	1	2	3	4	Excessive punishments are counterproductive

Now add up your scores and note your total on the continuum below:

Theory X   **Theory Y**
1   4   8   12   14   16   20   24   28   32

This activity is based on research carried out by behavioural psychologist Douglas McGregor. He recognised that there are two diametrically opposite ways of looking at the world and identified two extreme sets of assumptions that characterise each point of view. He called these opposing philosophies 'Theory X' and 'Theory Y'.

Theory X managers believe that people:

■ have an inborn dislike of work;
■ must be controlled, directed and threatened with punishment before they will make any sort of effort;
■ prefer to be told what to do and will avoid taking responsibility at all costs.

These managers are likely to rule by fear, by putting up barriers between management and the workforce and by giving orders and threatening punishment.

Theory Y managers believe that:

■ people enjoy physical and mental effort just as much as leisure activities or resting;
■ if they are committed to achieving something, people will exercise self-direction and self-control;
■ under the right conditions, people will accept and seek responsibility;
■ the vast majority of the population are capable of exercising imagination, creativity and ingenuity.

These managers are likely to take a positive view of others and will encourage responsibility and trust. McGregor found that Theory Y leaders tended to produce better results than Theory X leaders. Their subordinates showed higher creativity, more innovation and there were fewer staff problems.

Empowering managers believe that others *are* willing and able to take more responsibility for their own work. They believe that most people want to do a good job and that they gain just as much satisfaction from obtaining good results as they do from obtaining financial rewards. They also recognise that people cannot become empowered overnight; they need plenty of encouragement and support, especially if the approach is new to the department or team. They greet failure or mistakes, not with irritation and annoyance, but with renewed efforts to devise another solution to the problem.

Look again at your own Theory X assumptions – those for which you circled 1 or 2 on the above table. Is there anything you can do to make sure that you are not preventing your team members from giving of their best? For example:

■ Can you try allowing a group or an individual to take on a particular task within a clearly defined framework? If they have a measure of success, you might feel able to trust them more in future.

■ Try developing the skills of individuals who are already showing promise so that they will soon be able to take on more responsibility.

■ Could you be honest about some of the problems and issues that face the department or team as it strives to reach its targets? Allowing members to help identify the problems should also help them to participate in finding a solution.

creating effective working relationships

The difference between a lady and a flower girl is not how she behaves but how she is treated.

Pygmalion by George Bernard Shaw

Psychologists have now managed to demonstrate the 'Pygmalion Effect' in action. In one experiment, three teams of sales persons were given different briefings. The first team was told that managers have high expectations of its performance, the second was told that expectations were average and the third was told that expectations were low. Whereas the top group showed an outstanding performance, the bottom group performed even worse than predicted. But the middle group refused to accept the mediocre label that had been imposed upon them and showed marked and unexpected overall improvements.

You probably know the old saying 'treat people as you would like to be treated', and this is of course still important. But to cause a real transformation you should treat others as though they were *already* the people you would like them to become.

If you aim to develop an environment within which greater empowerment can take place, you may need to reconsider your relationships with the people in your team.

To develop an effective working relationship with them you must:

■ *Respect them:* this means valuing them for what they are – for the unique qualities that give them their individuality. Respect is not about friendship or having mutual likes or dislikes – you might respect someone you do not like or be friends with someone you don't respect.

■ *Show empathy:* letting people know that you can see things from their point of view can help them to gain a clearer picture of problems and issues from their own frames of reference rather than from yours.

■ *Be sincere:* this means being yourself and being honest about your feelings and opinions. It also involves communicating to other people that you are open to new ideas and want to help.

If you combine them, these three factors will help you to create relationships based on openness and trust; relationships that will increase others' confidence and enable them to take on more responsibility.

Think about your own experience of working relationships and the effects they have had on your performance. Give an example of a poor working relationship that prevented you from giving of your best.

_____

_____

_____

_____

Now identify a good relationship that contributed to the overall effectiveness of the task you were trying to achieve.

_____

_____

_____

_____

You may have discovered that the quality of your working relationships directly affects your motivation and your ability to commit yourself to a particular task.

Good relationships empower people because they:

- encourage regular and open communication;
- ensure that everyone's suggestions will be listened to and considered;
- allow people to admit any lack of expertise, secure in the knowledge that support will be provided for any shortfall.

Poor relationships hinder empowerment because they lead to:

- an unwillingness to keep others informed about developments and progress;
- hostility and distrust between individuals, which may prevent the right people from working together;
- difficulties in making decisions because conflicts cannot be resolved;
- frustration and loss of morale.

Managers who want to empower people try to create relationships in which team members feel valued, where they are able to take risks and where they learn how to be confident. They do this by:

- appreciating what team members achieve;
- being open and honest;
- taking a positive attitude;
- encouraging people.

It is only with the development of trust that team members can feel safe enough to move away from the comfort of the known and risk taking a step into the unknown. If they have enough trust in you, they will be able to afford the gamble of making mistakes as they put their ideas into practice. If you can't trust them and react by punishing their mistakes, you will raise barriers which will damage your ability to empower in the future and the team's ability to become more involved.

creating adult-to-adult relationships

It is bad enough that we treat children like children, but is it really necessary to treat adults like children as well?

Team Leadership Trainer

In many organisations, managerial and supervisory behaviour is based on the parental pattern – either directive and authoritarian or condescending and protective. We feel that we must tell people precisely what we want done and then patronise them if they succeed or punish them if they fail. But unless the members of today's well-educated workforce are treated as equals and shown that they are appreciated, they simply won't produce what they are capable of producing.

Transactional Analysis is a way of analysing and describing human behaviour that was developed in the late 1950s by Eric Berne, a Californian psychiatrist. TA provides a vocabulary that can help us to understand and improve our relationships with the people we manage.

Berne believed that everyone's personality has three different dimensions which he called 'states of mind'. Each state of mind is characterised by different ways of feeling, speaking and behaving, and we are all capable of assuming each one of them at different times. He names these states Parent, Adult and Child. Berne's use of these words is related to the way we use them in everyday life but it is not identical to this common usage:

- Concepts associated with the *Parent* are: orders, authority, directive, teacher, warm, caring, critical, concern, taking care.
- Concepts associated with the *Adult* are: rational, logical, mature, unemotional, dull, sensible, forward thinking, analytical, responsible, reliable.
- Concepts associated with the *Child* are: fun, rebellious, spontaneous, cute, manipulative, sly, accepting, trusting, irresponsible, emotional.

In the Berne model, the Parent concept is divided into two groups, which he called Critical Parent and Nurturing Parent:

■ The *Critical Parent* gives orders, wags the finger and criticises.
■ The *Nurturing Parent* is warm, caring and full of concerns for others.

The Child state was also subdivided, this time into three different groups – Natural Child, Adapted Child and Manipulative Child (Little Professor):

■ The *Natural Child* is irresponsible, fun loving, uninhibited and innocent.
■ The *Adapted Child* is either compliant, apologetic and whingeing or alternatively can be rebellious, defiant and negative.
■ The *Manipulative Child* is hesitant, cute, sly and selfish.

Berne observed that each of us is capable of assuming any of these six states in our relations with other people. However, we may have a tendency to adopt one way of acting more often than another, or certain situations or individuals may push us into a particular style of behaviour.

The process of describing behaviours in terms of these three states of mind is called transactional analysis because it involves *analysing the transactions* between people in terms of whether they are:

$$\text{Parent} \longleftrightarrow \text{Child}$$
$$\text{Child} \longleftrightarrow \text{Child}$$
$$\text{Adult} \longleftrightarrow \text{Adult}$$
$$\text{Adult} \longleftrightarrow \text{Child}$$

... and so on.

The ideal transaction in an empowering relationship is *Adult* to *Adult* – because these relationships are open and based on mutual respect and equality. But there may be times when things go wrong and an *Adapted Child* needs a *Nurturing Parent*. Or there may be occasions when a team needs a *Natural Child* to bring some spontaneity, creativity or fun into the proceedings.

Real problems can occur when a person is locked into a particular style or when the transaction is crossed, for example:

A says: 'There's a vacancy in the team taking the exhibition to Wembley this year. How do you feel about going?'
B replies: 'Oh, you're always trying to load extra responsibility onto me, why do I always get picked on? It's all too much. I can't cope any more.'

Here 'A' spoke as Adult to Adult, and the reply was Adapted Child to Critical Parent. The situation is unlikely to resolve itself until 'B' is ready to relate to 'A' as an Adult.

Some people, usually unwittingly, adopt a particular style in order to manipulate the behaviour of others. The style adopted by one person during a transaction can force another into taking on a particular role.

For example, if:

A talks to B as an *Adult*
B replies as a *Child*
A is forced to respond as a *Parent*.

Or if:

C relates to D as a *Parent*
D can find him or herself behaving like a *Child*.

Remember that all of us can act from all of these states, given the right circumstances and attitude at the time. For example, five different ways of trying to correct a team member's lack of punctuality might be:

■ 'This is just not good enough. You have been late four times this week and people are being kept waiting because of you'.
Your finger is wagging and you are in **Critical Parent**.

■ 'You're terribly late again you know. Tell me, is there something wrong?'
You are trying to comfort the person by finding excuses for the lateness. You are in **Nurturing Parent**.

■ 'You are late again. Shall we sit down and discuss why this is happening? Then perhaps we can work towards a solution.'
Here you are treating the latecomer as an Adult and you are in **Adult** *yourself.*

■ 'Late again but who cares!? It's my birthday and I'm taking the rest of the day off anyway!'
You sweep by, singing and smiling with not a care in the world for unimportant details like punctuality. You are in **Natural Child**.

■ 'I'm so glad you're late this morning! It means you probably won't mind staying on a bit later tonight to help me finish the end of quarter performance reports.'
A sly glint comes into your eye as you work out how to use the situation to your advantage. You are in **Manipulative Child**.

Spend some time observing the transactions that take place around you. Try to identify examples of the three principle states of mind. Notice the words and actions that indicated that the person was in the state of mind that you identified.

Transactional Analysis can provide you – and your colleagues – with a useful language for describing the relationships between you. It should also develop your understanding of the kinds of transactions you should aim for if you want to empower others – usually adult-to-adult relationships.

leading by example

> The story goes that in 1943 a battalion of soldiers was lined up waiting to be inspected by General Montgomery. It was raining and, although the officers wore raincoats, the troops had none and they were soaked. When Montgomery's car pulled up he stepped out, wearing a raincoat. He took a few steps, stopped, went back to the car, took his coat off and returned to carry out the inspection. The troops cheered.

We started this chapter by discussing your beliefs about people. But actions, as they say, speak louder than words, so it is vital to be a good role model for the people you want to empower.

What you do as team leader or manager sends clear messages to the people around you. After all, the only evidence other people have of your commitment to empowerment is how you behave. And you can be sure that everything you say and everything you do will be noted and judged by the people who are responsible to you.

There are many ways for managers to provide a good example for their teams – perhaps putting on overalls and working alongside production operatives to get a feel for how well a particular process is working or abolishing the senior managers' car park and the directors' washroom. Whatever you decide to do in practical terms, it is vital to model the behaviours that you want others to adopt:

- ■ if you want them to do what they say they will do – you will have to prove yourself to be reliable;
- ■ if you want them to be innovative – you will have to be prepared to take risks;
- ■ if you want others to make an extra effort – you will have to push yourself harder;
- ■ if you want them to be open – you will have to be honest and sincere yourself;
- ■ if you want them to trust each other – you will have to trust them;
- ■ if you want them to perform miracles – you will have to provide them with a positive, exciting and inspiring vision of the future.

Your example will reinforce the habits you want to enforce and help weed out the ones you want to eliminate. Think about your behaviours at work – how can you lead by example? Suggest some ideas in the space below.

_____

_____

_____

_____

We can't, of course, know which behaviours you will concentrate on modelling. But here is what other managers said when we asked them what 'leading by example' means to them:

'I only have one rule for my team – you can do anything I do.' 'I make sure I am seen. I talk to people regularly and work alongside them occasionally.'

'You can't expect others to think of new ideas if you never have a creative thought yourself.'

'Trust people – and nine times out of ten they will repay your trust.'

'I set high standards for myself and make it clear that I expect the same of others.'

This chapter has focused on the need to create effective relationships and a culture in which people will feel secure enough to take on new responsibilities. The next deals with communications: providing people with information and making sure that you are receptive to the messages that others are sending to you.

knowledge is power

Nothing is worse for morale than keeping people in the dark. If you don't tell them, for instance, about those plans for reorganisation, about the new equipment that is about to be installed – and if you don't tell them how well they are doing – you can hardly expect them to become excited about changes, get involved in solving problems or relish the idea of taking on new tasks.

This chapter aims to help you minimise the 'nobody ever tells me anything' syndrome. To empower people you have to communicate like you have never communicated before, and that means asking questions and listening as well as providing information yourself. People cannot be empowered unless they know what it is they are supposed to become involved in.

providing information

Providing other people with high quality information is one of the keys to helping them develop their independence. Often the information you impart will help people to make decisions; for example, how to increase productivity, how to eliminate excessive errors or how to make sure that customers know about complaints procedures. At other times, the information will be more directive; for example, the new health and safety policy or details about a forthcoming merger.

This is what one manager said when asked why he shares as much information as possible with his workforce:

> You can't expect individuals to take responsibility unless they have the information to make decisions and take action. But if you do give information to individuals, they cannot help *but* take responsibility.
> *Building Society Area Manager*

These are just some of the items of information that are relevant and necessary if you want people to be more involved in decision making:

- productivity figures for particular periods;
- data on profitability;
- customer satisfaction information;
- details about customer complaints in relation to a particular product;
- advance information about strategic decisions that have been made by the company;
- information about competitor activity;
- health and safety statistics;
- how the team/department/unit is performing in relation to agreed targets;
- results of market research surveys;
- feedback on research into staff morale;
- reports on vehicle maintenance problems;
- figures showing sales linked to a special promotion.

Many managers believe that the simple fact of publishing this kind of data has a dramatic effect on motivation.

A foreman in an engineering factory took to writing productivity figures in chalk on the shop floor after every shift. Soon the various shifts started competing with each other and productivity increased dramatically.

More and more evidence is showing that people actually have a thirst for knowledge and will make every effort to understand the implications of information that is directly relevant to their work and their ultimate well-being.

But of course we are not saying that confidential information should be made public. It would be unthinkable, for example, for everyone in the organisation to have access to other people's personnel records and there will be many occasions when the discussion of commercially sensitive strategies must be confined to the boardroom.

In general, however, making information available to everyone is important for a number of reasons:

- it confirms that you view people as partners in problem solving and decision making
- it enables people to contribute to continuous improvement
- it stirs up competition – and most people would rather see performance figures improve than deteriorate
- it spurs people to ask questions and prompts the collection of more information
- it helps to shift responsibility to the front line
- it improves communication between different departments or teams.

presenting information

However good your information is, it will be of little use to anyone at all if it is not presented effectively. Many people, consciously or unconsciously, feel that they are suffering from an 'information crisis'. Paradoxically, this can mean too much information, and, at the same time, too little. It is no good providing people with too much of the kind of information that swamps them with irrelevant detail, and too little information which is accurate, timely and relevant.

To be useful, information should meet the following criteria:

1. **It should be relevant.**
   Incomplete information means that decision makers have to work in the dark. Irrelevant information, on the other hand, wastes time, obscures the vital facts, congests the information channels and increases administrative costs.

> Employees in one large organisation take the advice about sharing information so much to heart that they regularly make over 20 copies of every single e-mail and send these to everyone who might be remotely affected or interested. The result is that a large number of people find themselves reading them unnecessarily.

2. **It should be supplied in appropriate detail.**
   One consequence of new technology is that more information is available than is strictly necessary. This means that you have to consider carefully what level of detail is required by the people to whom you are providing the information.
3. **It should be accurate.**
   Inaccurate information leads to poor decision making. However, the expense of achieving a high degree of accuracy must be balanced against the expected benefits.

4. **It should be complete.**

   Like accuracy, completeness can only be judged in relative terms. It would make no sense to hold up a vital decision because the information required was not yet complete in every last detail.

5. **It should be timely.**

   Again, because of the need to react quickly to changing circumstances, it may sometimes be better to have information now that is slightly less accurate rather than wait until later for a higher, and perhaps unnecessary, degree of precision.

6. **It should be effectively presented.**

   However sound the information, it is less than useful if it arrives unsorted or badly presented. Research has shown that information is most easily assimilated if it is presented in the form of tables, charts or graphs. Consider the following three ways of presenting the same information:

   a) Our current target is to achieve 20 per cent of market share by the year end. In the first quarter we achieved 16 per cent, the second quarter saw a slight rise to 18 per cent and in this, the third quarter, our market share has increased by only 0.5 per cent, bringing our total achievement so far up to 18.5 per cent. If this trend continues we envisage an end of year figure of about 19.5 per cent.

   b) Performance against market share target of 20 per cent:
      - first quarter: 16 per cent;
      - second quarter: 18 per cent;
      - third quarter: 18.5 per cent;
      - projected figure for last quarter: 19.5 per cent.

   c) Turnover:

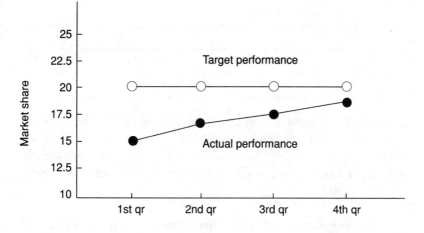

Most people would agree that the simple graph has most impact and gives the information in the form that is most immediate and user-friendly. You will find it useful to consider how you can use graphics to convey both simple and complex information.

the importance of two-way communication

Although it is true that 'management' memos, reports, notices, newsletters, presentations and briefings have their place in an organisation's communications network, these systems form only one half of this important process. Successful organisations make sure that information flows upwards as well as downwards – by asking for information, by listening carefully, by allowing people to bounce ideas off each other and by listening for non-verbal messages.

How do you gather information from the people who work with you?

Organisations have introduced a number of devices for making sure that communication is and remains a two-way process. Here are a selection of practical ideas, which range from simply putting a box on the wall to redesigning the entire working environment:

- ■ *Suggestion schemes:* these have been much maligned in the past, usually because they have been introduced as a panacea to solve all employee relations problems. Nevertheless, they should not be dismissed out of hand; if they are properly handled they are a quick way of encouraging people to contribute ideas.
- ■ *Blackboards and flipcharts:* physical 'trappings' such as these can help to inspire regular informal information sharing between groups of people who may not otherwise meet on a routine basis. Many people are used to having these items in the training room as a way of noting down and communicating their ideas, but it is not so common to see them in the corner of an office, on the shopfloor or in the coffee room.
- ■ *Changing the furniture:* a simple idea that one manager introduced was to exchange the four-person round tables in the canteen for long rectangular tables that would seat up to 12 people. The rationale for this move was that strangers are more likely to come into contact at a larger table, whereas at the small table four friends might sit and have lunch together every day.

▓ *Organising inter-lunch meetings:* these are a chance for members of the top management team in large organisations to meet over lunch with employees from all levels and areas of the business. In one organisation between 15 and 30 people attend each lunch with one or two managers. Each manager aims to do six such events each year, meaning that ideally, around 1200 people each year have the chance to talk directly with a senior manager.

▓ *Creating a flexible office space:* the example which follows illustrates how communication flows can be enhanced and productivity can be improved when managers are smart enough to involve the workforce in planning their own office space.

---

the fourth generation office

In his book *Managing in the next Millennium*, Mike Johnson describes an office that has been designed by the 60-person team at Digital Equipment in Finland. The first generation office was simply an office; in the second generation everyone had his/her own office; in the third generation, offices had become open plan to encourage communication. In fact the open plan experiment failed because it caused too much noise and stress to allow for good productivity.

In this fourth generation office there are people pacing the rooms with cordless phones, reading or consulting a computer screen from the comfort of a reclining chair, or discussing projects over a cup of coffee in the relaxation room. In a corner there is some garden furniture and a garden swing for meetings of up to four people.

There are 35 work spaces for 60 people, with no assigned desks (this is known as 'hot desking'). Management sits in the same room, not hidden away.

According to Digital, the unique feature is not the physical layout, but the fact that the concept resolves around communication and flexibility. First, the sales and service people should be out talking to customers so you don't need one desk per person. Second, people in the office should be communicating, not tied to their desk because their phone is there. When the office was built it provided the world's biggest installation of portable phones.

Third, people like to work in different environments, so there are meeting rooms, traditional desk space and lounge areas. Each employee works in the way he or she is most comfortable.

Source: *Managing in the Next Millennium* by Mike Johnson, Butterworth–Heinemann 1995, pp 131–132.

But these are all just techniques – clever mechanisms, if you like, for generating and collecting ideas. The fact remains that the basic task of management, whatever the working environment, is to use that most fundamental of all empowering communication skills: simply listening to what others are saying.

the importance of listening and questioning

By listening we mean not just hearing words and sentences, but making a real effort to understand what another person is saying to you. Of all the skills that you use in communicating, listening is probably the most important of all. Unfortunately most of us are not natural listeners; we find output easier than input. Signs of a poor listener are jumping to conclusions, interrupting people, finishing others' sentences and letting the mind wander.

Note down any problems you have with listening in the space below.

_____

_____

_____

_____

If you make a point of asking people what they think and of actively listening to what they say, you will help to make them feel that they can contribute something of value to the work of the department or team and the business as a whole.

A good way of making sure you are really listening is to train yourself to ask effective questions. One of the most common types of questions are 'closed questions'. They are closed because, rather than allowing the other person to make a full answer, they usually demand either a yes/no answer (Were you... ? Have you... ?) or specific information (How far... ? How much... ?). Closed questions are valuable because they can draw out specific information or facts. However, their main drawback is that they do not allow any further discussion, expansion or qualification. Furthermore, using too many closed questions sometimes seems like prying, and this can feel threatening for the person on the receiving end. Closed questions put you in control of the situation in a very obvious way, and this may not be the best strategy for developing empowering relationships.

Open questions on the other hand, encourage people to express, explore and develop their opinions, ideas and attitudes. Here are some examples of the types of questions that you might use to help others to solve a problem:

- What have you done about this so far?
- Why did you choose that strategy?
- What results did that produce?
- What other options are open to you?
- Which of these seems the most feasible?
- Who else can help us solve this problem?

Try changing these rather threatening closed questions into more empowering open ones:

1. Have you got any idea how to improve this?
2. I'm going to be a bit pushed this week. Can you help with the monthly report?
3. Do you know why the absence rate is so high this quarter?
4. My idea is to have a meeting with our key customers at least once a quarter. What do you think?
5. Do you want to enter the teamworking competition? It would raise our national profile considerably.

paying attention

Listening to the replies to your questions is not just a passive process but one that should involve you in concentrating hard, so that you hear not only *what* the person is saying, but *how* they say it. Showing that you are paying attention by adopting positive body language helps to meet a speaker's need to feel valued and respected. This can actually help you to listen more attentively.

- ▓ *Your eye-contact* should not be a fixed stare but a friendly gaze. If you find it difficult to maintain eye contact, try looking at the spot half way between the eyebrows.
- ▓ *Your posture* (the way you hold yourself as you sit or stand) should indicate that the person doing the talking is now at the centre of your attention. You will give the wrong impression if you turn away or slouch.
- ▓ *Space between you and the talker* If there is too much, this might imply that you are trying to distance yourself from what is being said.
- ▓ *Your mannerisms* should create the appropriate impression. Pen clicking, hair twirling and rattling the change in your pocket, for example, can be very

distracting for someone who is trying to communicate with you.

Even once we have grasped the importance of body language, it is still not an easy task to control it and prevent unintended messages from confusing the other person. What messages might the following managers be giving to the people they should be listening to?

1. When Huw is hearing the production team give their presentation, he looks at his watch four times in the space of ten minutes.

   _____

   _____

   _____

   _____

2. When Hannah is having a conversation with her assistant she looks to see who is coming in every time the door of the open plan office opens.

   _____

   _____

   _____

   _____

3. Nigel sits bolt upright in his chair during the team meeting.

   _____

   _____

   _____

   _____

4. Maisie drums her fingers on the desk when the maintenance crew come in to explain about some major difficulties with the new computer system.

_____

_____

_____

_____

To listen more effectively you will need to develop a number of qualities, including:

- **Concentrating:** this means putting all other thoughts out of your mind and thinking consciously about what the person is saying.
- **Patience:** poor listeners tend to interrupt with another question before the person has finished talking. Try to keep a tight rein on your enthusiasm and allow people to speak at their own pace.
- **Objectivity:** good listeners refrain from making a judgement until they have heard everything that the other person has to say.

making meetings empowering

Meetings are a vital tool for informing and empowering people. Unfortunately, unless they are carefully considered and planned in advance, they can also be a time-wasting and frustrating experience for all concerned. Think of some meetings that you have attended recently.

First, consider one where participants emerged smiling, animated and ready for action. What happened in the meeting to make them react like that?

_____

_____

_____

_____

Next, consider a meeting from which participants emerged looking disgruntled, angry, tired or bored. What happened in the meeting to make them react that way?

_____

_____

_____

Empowering meetings don't just happen, they have to be worked at – not only by the person leading or chairing them but also by the people who participate. But before you can start to improve the effectiveness of the meetings you organise or take part in, it is important to clarify the reasons why meetings occur at all.

If a meeting has no real purpose it should not take place. That seems like a trite statement, but it is surprising how many gatherings happen just out of habit, or because people do not feel confident enough to make a decision without calling everyone in. There are two main purposes for the meetings that take place in business organisations, and all agenda items will ultimately relate to one of them:

1. to provide information; and
2. to make decisions.

But meetings can also serve a number of other valuable purposes:

■ *They can give participants a sense of group identity.* Feeling that they are part of a team with a common purpose and shared goals gives many people more confidence to undertake new tasks.

■ *They can enhance motivation and commitment.* Being involved in a discussion, contributing ideas and ultimately arriving at decisions as a group helps people to feel a sense of ownership towards those decisions.

■ *They can help to develop synergy.* In effective meetings people become more creative than they would if they were working on their own. This means that the team can achieve things that would simply not be possible for isolated individuals.

■ *They provide an opportunity for positive reinforcement.* It is possible to reinforce desired behaviours by publicly recognising achievements and celebrating individual and team success.

Below are listed seven key criteria for transforming meetings from dull routine gatherings into enjoyable and empowering experiences:

1. **They should be planned and prepared well in advance.** This seems an obvious point, but unfortunately it is rarely adequately observed. However, if you do allow participants time to suggest items for the agenda, to read the notes from the last meeting and to prepare the points they want to make, everyone will feel more involved in the ensuing discussion – and more committed to action points that eventually emerge.

2. **Everyone should be aware of the purpose or objectives of the meeting.** Again, this simple point is all too often omitted from business meetings. Yet it is amazing how much more effective they can be when everyone is

aware of the expected outcome. If the point is not clarified by the start of the meeting, it should become the first agenda item.

3. **The time available should be appropriately structured.** Again, if this has not been decided beforehand, you should start the proceedings by allotting a certain amount of time to each agenda item. This will help everyone to agree and clarify the relative priorities of the different points. The person leading the meeting should encourage everyone to be brief so that the time deadlines are achieved.

4. **Participants should be encouraged to communicate effectively.** It is often left to the person chairing the meeting to ask for clarification, to summarise or to check for understanding or agreement. But if all participants see it as part of their responsibility to do these things for the group, the discussion will be more focused, less time will be wasted and fewer misunderstandings will occur.

5. **The meeting should be effectively facilitated.** A good 'chair' or facilitator can sometimes make the difference between an excellent meeting and a poor one. Such a person can keep everyone on track, eliminate repetition and ensure that everyone present has the opportunity to make a contribution.

    Encouraging the active participation of everyone, especially the ones who normally lack the confidence to speak in a group, is an important part of the role of the chair. There are a number of ways of involving participants more at meetings including:
    - breaking into pairs or groups for short periods to discuss particular issues;
    - rotating the chair – this way each member gets a turn eventually;
    - asking an individual or group to prepare a specific topic and then present it to the meeting;

- asking a member who has not contributed much to summarise discussions or to make notes on a flip-chart, whiteboard or OHP.

6. **Participants should review the effectiveness of the meeting.** It is useful to spend some time at the end of a meeting reviewing how it went. If participants are honest, they can provide feedback and ideas that will improve things the next time. To do this properly it would be useful to agree some 'success indicators' against which participants can review their performance.

For example, people may agree that the meeting will have been successful if it:
- starts and finishes on time;
- gives everyone a chance to contribute;
- achieves its objectives; and so on.

If some of these criteria are not met, part of the review could focus on how to remedy the situation next time.

7. **Meetings should lead to action.** The approach adopted during meetings will tend to influence the behaviour of the team when it is apart; a good meeting will inspire people to go away and give their all to their allotted tasks. Nevertheless, this enthusiasm may wane in time, and it can be useful to adopt some methods of helping people to feel involved and to cooperate fully outside meetings. Some of these strategies are:
- at the end of a meeting, planning carefully the details of what everyone agrees to do before the next one;
- reviewing the previous meeting's action plan at the beginning of the next one;
- delegating responsibility for planning and carrying out particular tasks to sub-groups or working parties;

- making sure that members keep in touch with each other and are kept up to date with important information that affects the work of the team;
- networking with members of other teams in order to learn from their successes and problems.

None of the above strategies will work if they are not underpinned by a sense of shared purpose, an atmosphere of support and trust and clear procedures for making decisions. All these 'building blocks' must be in place before true empowerment can occur.

better briefings

Briefings are similar to normal meetings except that their focus tends to be on sharing information rather than on solving problems and making decisions. They have become widely adopted by large organisations as a way of keeping the workforce in touch with what is happening outside their immediate workplace. They focus attention on the broader and more long-term issues rather than confining this to operational problems or routine tasks:

> We run sessions every month on a different theme – keeping people informed, telling them about service performance, briefing them on changes and the new services.
>
> *Personnel manager*

The briefing methods you might select include:

- ▓ face-to-face – in a large gathering or privately with a small group or an individual;
- ▓ in writing – in an e-mail, newsletter, poster or information sheet;
- ▓ on the telephone;
- ▓ a combination of the above methods.

The problem with briefings is that, unless you are very careful, they can go on too long, they can wander off the point and they can leave people feeling less rather than more empowered.

Do your briefings:	Yes	No
finish on time?	☐	☐
keep to the point?	☐	☐
enable people to ask questions or contribute in some way?	☐	☐
include topics that are relevant for everyone who attends?	☐	☐
leave people satisfied that the time spent in the briefing was well spent?	☐	☐

Briefings should entail more than just giving out information. They are an ideal opportunity to involve people, to share responsibility and to increase enthusiasm and commitment. If your briefings are not as empowering as you would like them to be, consider how you can improve them:

- Can you make a point of explaining the purpose of the briefing clearly at the beginning and summarising what has been said or decided at the end?
- Can you try making your own inputs brief, clear and to the point and seeking inputs from other people?
- Is it possible to finish by asking for questions, agreeing follow-up actions and the time of the next briefing?

It will be easier to make other people feel more motivated if you present information enthusiastically and positively. Your team will take its lead from you – if you show that you are willing to take on responsibility for making things work they will do so too.

walking the job

Walking the job means getting out from behind a desk, not to give orders and ask for progress reports so much as to listen to people and to observe what is happening in the workplace. Your relationship is that of an equal partner in achieving the goals and objectives of the business:

> They know better than I do what the problems are. They have probably thought of many of the solutions as well if we only think to ask. It's time consuming keeping in daily contact with all our drivers and technicians, but that's what the job's about at the end of the day.
>
> *Operations manager*

When you walk around the site, the shopfloor or the office you will take the opportunity to observe and ask questions:

- How's it going?
- Any problems?
- How are you getting on with that new process/piece of equipment?
- That looks good. How did you do it?
- How's the family?

Walking the job is not just relevant for front line managers. *All* managers need direct information about what is happening on the production line and at the interface with customers. It's a valuable opportunity to gather information, monitor the situation, create friendships and build up a picture of what it's like to be 'doing the job'. Furthermore, by getting out there and seeing people for yourself, you will be helping to reduce the 'them and us' attitude that so often prevades organisations.

In other words, walking the job is a powerful tool for communicating informally with the workforce and for making everyone feel part of the wider business. It is important to build these visits into your daily routine – especially if you find the personal approach difficult.

Although the object of walking the job regularly is to observe, to listen and to praise, you can also use the opportunity to ask people interesting and motivating questions which may result in them becoming more involved or thinking of new ideas.

Make a point of walking the job regularly during the next month. It is a good idea to take a notebook with you and jot down the things you observe or hear, or the action points that occur to you on the way round. You may like to use these questions as a guide:

1. What is going well?
2. What are the difficulties?
3. What are you not happy with?
4. What is your view of how things should be in the section/department and in your part of it?
5. What needs to be tackled that gets in the way of you doing your job properly?
6. If you had *carte blanche*, how would you change things for the better?
7. How can I help?

At the end of the month, review the information you have gained by talking and listening to people in this way. It is important to follow up this activity by taking appropriate action:

■ Are there any problems that you can fix easily?
■ Which issues do you need to refer up the line to other managers?
■ How and when will you report back to the team on responses received from elsewhere?
■ Would any of the problems you found lend themselves to a focus group or quality circle?
■ If a quality circle seems appropriate, how will you encourage this approach?

■ What support will you give? Where can you find support and information yourself?
■ How can you give feedback on what you saw during the month's walkabout?
■ How can you say 'thank you' for work well done?

In this way you not only empower people, you also build a network and gain a wider appreciation of the situation that people are in and the key issues that face them.

This chapter has explored the communication skills and techniques that are required of an empowering manager. The next one turns to look at the part of your role that involves developing others.

helping people to learn

People need development if they are to be capable of taking on new tasks and responsibilities. Lifelong learning, acquiring information, widening their experience, building up their confidence and self-esteem: these are the basic building blocks of empowerment. But it's no good training everybody in everything (at great expense) and hoping that they will be able to retain something useful. They won't. The development that you do should be relevant, flexible and delivered at the right time.

This chapter is concerned with how you can use development to help empower people.

a learner's point of view

By reading this book you are learning how to empower other people. You probably know exactly why you decided to undertake this study and you have taken on the responsibility for what you learn and how you learn it. This experience as a learner is invaluable when you are working as a facilitator or 'learning manager' with others. It will help you to counteract the common tendency for teachers and trainers to think only of what they are going to do and to forget to consider what the experience feels like from the point of view of the learners on the receiving end.

Try to recall a recent learning experience that was successful and enjoyable for you. Think of any kind of experience – it does not have to be a taught course or set programme of study.

1. What did you learn?

_____

_____

_____

_____

2. Why did you decide to learn this?

_____

_____

_____

_____

3. Where did you learn this?

_____

_____

_____

_____

4. How did you learn?

_____

_____

_____

_____

5. Who helped you to learn?

_____

_____

_____

_____

6. How do you feel about the experience?

_____

_____

_____

_____

Your experience may go at least some way to confirming the findings of many other people involved in developing others – that adults learn best when:

- they choose to learn something;
- they have a definite motivation for learning;
- the environment is informal and non-threatening;
- their previous experiences and achievements are recognised and built on;
- they have some control over how and when they learn
- they participate actively in the learning;
- they have opportunities to apply what they have learnt;
- they receive appropriate help and support.

In other words, people will not develop successfully if you send them on a course that has no immediate relevance, if you fail to ask them how much of the subject matter they know already, if you put them in an uncomfortable room, if you ask them to listen to a lecture that lasts an hour (or more), or if you give them no help or encouragement whatsoever! Put like that, it sounds most unlikely, but some of these things do happen in real life.

the responsibilities of learners

If everyone could become a brain surgeon, an engineer or a professional athlete by watching a snappy video, taking a course or reading a book, we'd certainly see some rapid upheaval in our society!
Leadership Skills for Every Manager
by Jim Clemner and Art McNeil

It is most important that you mirror the process of empowerment in the development that you carry out with learners. You must encourage them to take responsibility for their own learning, to make their own choices and to become independent learners. This is because when people are fully involved they are more motivated, they remember more and they will be more likely to want to continue learning in the future. This concept of 'autonomous learning' shifts the focus from the teacher on to the learner, so that successful learning becomes the priority rather than how the subject matter is taught or who teaches it.

The concept also carries an implicit recognition that learning is an active process – that people cannot sit like empty receptacles waiting for a teacher to come along and fill them up with knowledge. Learners are not able to retain knowledge or learn new skills unless they become actively involved during the process of learning. Imagine trying to learn how to drive if you were never allowed to sit behind the wheel or take a car out on the road. How could you learn the highway code if no-one ever pointed out the various signs or discussed the implications of the rules of the road?

Unfortunately, many people's experience in the education system has not prepared them for these responsibilities and these approaches. They may well resist your efforts to get them to become more active and involved. The implication is that you may have to work with people who want you to organise everything for them.

how to develop people

The development method that most of us are familiar with is the training programme – usually away from the job. However, it is now recognised that expensive courses are not the only or even the best way of enabling people to learn. A virtually unlimited number of valuable learning opportunities are available within the workplace itself. Generally, people are more empowered by development that occurs 'on the job' than they would be by going on courses. This is because they will learn more quickly and effectively if what they are doing is practical and immediately relevant.

This is not to say that formal training courses have no part to play in helping people to learn. You may decide that members of your team need some conventional training to meet identified needs. Although courses make a valuable contribution, you will find that developing people in the workplace is useful because:

■ it is inexpensive;
■ it is easy to organise;
■ you can get involved yourself;
■ it is flexible.

Managers have found the following opportunities for development useful:

■ getting people involved in special projects;
■ shadowing – allowing someone to follow an experienced worker for a specified period of time;
■ one-to-one coaching;
■ in-house workshops;

- ■ on-the-job training by an experienced worker – often called 'sitting by Nellie';
- ■ delegating some of their own tasks;
- ■ arranging for two people to swap jobs for a while;
- ■ seconding people into other departments;
- ■ suggesting that people read things (technical manuals, journal articles, self-study workbooks like this one);
- ■ giving people the opportunity to cover their line manager's job when the latter is off sick or on holiday;
- ■ asking individual members to take turns to chair team meetings;
- ■ organising visits to other work areas – including customers and suppliers;
- ■ encouraging and supporting team and individual work in the community;
- ■ organising focus groups to find out what customers think.

Some of the methods in this list will be appropriate for some people and not for others. The method you choose in any instance will depend on the development need and the individuals involved. Often you will use a combination of methods, such as a coaching session followed by delegation – or visits followed by secondment. The important thing is not to restrict yourself to a limited range of methods but to consider all the resources available to you.

When selecting methods for developing people, you will find it useful to be aware of the advantages and disadvantages of each one. Think about these now in relation to:

1. Coaching

_____

_____

_____

_____

2. Sitting by Nellie

_____

_____

_____

_____

3. Shadowing

_____

_____

_____

_____

4. Delegation

_____

_____

_____

_____

Being aware of possible difficulties and drawbacks will help you when you are planning these development opportunities.

learning preferences

Different people prefer to learn in different ways – they have different learning styles. You only have to ask friends or colleagues how they learnt something and you will get a variety of answers:

> I like to teach myself through trial and error and by starting from first principles. I bought a new computer recently and worked out how to use it just by playing around with it. I only need to look at the instruction book when I come up against a problem I can't solve.
>
> *Ross, graphic designer*

I like to learn from experts. I haven't got the patience to read books on the whole – I learn best when someone demonstrates for me and I can ask questions.

Kris, apprentice hairdresser

I've been learning French for three years and my teacher tells me I'm quite good. Recently someone suggested that I should accompany one of our French speaking buyers on a trip to France. But I want to study a lot more before I will feel ready to put my knowledge to any practical use.

Sheila, personal assistant

Peter Honey and Alan Mumford have carried out research which suggests that most of us use a blend of four learning styles:

- *Activists* – who rely on doing. They involve themselves fully in new experiences. They are open-minded, not sceptical, and this tends to make them enthusiastic about anything new. Their philosophy is 'I'll try anything once'. They revel in short-term crisis fire-fighting and like to tackle problems by brainstorming. They often thrive on the challenge of new experiences but are bored with implementation and longer-term consolidation.
- *Reflectors* – who rely on watching. They like to stand back to ponder experiences and observe them from many different perspectives. They collect data first-hand and from others and prefer to chew it over thoroughly before coming to any conclusion. Their philosophy is to be cautious, to leave no stone unturned. In meetings they tend to adopt a low profile and have a slightly distant, tolerant, unruffled air about them – they listen to others and get the drift before making their own points.
- *Theorists* – who rely on thinking. They adapt and integrate observations into complex but logically

sound theories and think problems through step-by-step. They tend to be perfectionists, who will not rest until things are tidy and fit into their overall rational scheme. Their philosophy prizes rationality and logic – 'If it's logical, it's good'.

■ *Pragmatists* – who rely on feeling. They are keen on trying out new ideas, theories and techniques to see if they work in practice. They are the sort of people who come back from management courses brimming over with new ideas they want to try out. They like to get on with things and act quickly and confidently on ideas that attract them. They tend to be impatient with 'beating around the bush' and with open-ended discussions. Their philosophy is: 'There is always a better way' and 'If it works, it's good'.

Which of the development methods we identified above do you think would best suit people with these different learning styles?

Activists

_____

_____

_____

_____

Reflectors

_____

_____

_____

_____

Theorists

_____

_____

_____

_____

Pragmatists

_____

_____

_____

_____

You will find it valuable to ask people how they prefer to learn when you are arranging development opportunities for them.

involving people in their development

Empowered people need:

- ▨ the work skills required to do the job;
- ▨ management skills such as planning, problem solving, decision making and data gathering;
- ▨ interpersonal skills like presenting information, listening and working with others.

As we saw at the beginning of this chapter, a crucial step in helping team members to become empowered is to involve them in their own development. You can start this process off by encouraging them to identify their own needs and to set their own goals. If they are not used to being asked what development they think they need, you may have to start the ball rolling by suggesting a few areas that you think would be useful. It is important that, whenever possible, people should have a say in planning their own development activities. Ideally, plans and goals should be negotiated between you and the individual concerned.

Whichever development method you agree with the learner, you want it to make an impact on the person's performance in their job and you want to ensure that it increases their ability to work independently. To get the best out of any training or development activity you need to:

■ *Make sure that people are well prepared for the development opportunity:* ideally people should have had some say in choosing the particular activity, but this is not always possible. You need to ensure that people are aware of the purpose of any training or development activity and they should understand how they stand to benefit from it. They should also have a good idea about the kind of experience that it will be and of what will be expected of them.

■ *Review what people have learnt:* one of the biggest difficulties with any learning experience is helping people to apply what they have learnt to the work situation. This is why reviewing is important. It is essential to put aside some time to talk over the experience with the person concerned. Encourage him or her to give you feedback on how it went, what happened, what he or she learnt and how the person felt about it. But just as important, look for chances to create situations where people can put what they have learnt into practice.

■ *Think about how the development could be followed up or extended:* there may be other development opportunities that follow on logically which either extend or reinforce the experience. Or there may be things people can do as part of their daily work which will help them to go further. The vital thing is that no development opportunity should be seen as an isolated experience; it is important to identify next steps and to make any arrangements necessary to make sure that they are taken.

coaching

One of the most efficient ways of getting the best out of the members of your team is to coach them. Some people think that coaching is the same as teaching or instructing, but any sports coach will tell you that it's much more than that. Coaches work on people's minds more than on practical skills or knowledge for its own sake. They build up confidence and self-esteem and help people to discover what they are really capable of. Of course, it is true that you need to learn skills if you are going to win a race, score a goal or achieve a target at work – but skills on their own are useless unless you have a positive mental attitude.

This is what some learners said about the experience of being coached:

'It makes you feel good.'
'It brings out the best in you.'
'It makes you realise how much you know already!'

Good managers have always coached their staff and you have almost certainly – perhaps without being aware of it – been coached by or coached other people at some time. Here are some examples of coaching activities:

- explaining and demonstrating a task, then getting learners to try while you watch;
- encouraging learners to watch someone else working and talking to them about it afterwards;
- observing learners doing their normal work, then sitting down with them and discussing strengths and areas for improvement;

- ■ giving learners new tasks or experiences; then, having discussed how these will be tacked, supporting them as they carry out these tasks;
- ■ asking learners about areas that are causing problems to find out what is causing them, then helping them to work out a solution, and later providing support while the solution is being put into practice;
- ■ analysing mistakes; inside every mistake are some lessons waiting to come out – the trick is to be non-judgmental and to discuss how to minimise the effects of the mistake and work out how to prevent it from happening again.

Coaching is nothing new. It traces its origins to the apprentice-ship system, where an older, more experienced worker passed his or her job skills and knowledge down to the younger gener-ation. Because coaching is done in the workplace, as part of everyone's everyday activities, it is less time-consuming than many other training and development methods. Other benefits are:

- ■ You can fit coaching sessions in with the other tasks you have to perform.
- ■ Because you are involved personally, you can make sure that appropriate learning takes place.
- ■ Coaching can give you the opportunity build a more open, honest and positive relationship with the people you work with.

For all these reasons coaching is probably the most powerful and cost-effective tool you have for developing and empow-ering your people.

Now plan how you will coach someone in your team.

What are the person's development needs?

_____

_____

_____

_____

When will you discuss the coaching opportunity with this person?

_____

_____

_____

_____

How will you coach the team member? (see above suggestions)

_____

_____

_____

_____

How will you support and monitor the person while he or she is learning?

_____

_____

_____

_____

Can anyone else contribute to coaching this individual?

_____

_____

_____

_____

You are not the only person who can act as a coach; look out for coaching potential in others and encourage them to develop these skills. Having a number of competent coaches in your department or team will greatly improve its effectiveness.

providing enabling support

Your job as a coach is to help people, wherever possible, to find their own ways of doing things because getting them to do things your way may:

- allow them to avoid thinking things through;
- reduce their sense of involvement in achieving goals and targets;
- lessen their sense of ownership of planned activities.

Table 4.1 contrasts the type of support that empowers people with that which will lead to dependency.

Table 4.1   *Types of support*

Empowering support:	Support that leads to dependency:
affirms what people can do	does things for people
encourages people to identify their own problems	takes people over or rescues them
deals with feelings of helplessness	confirms feelings of inadequacy
involves listening	gives advice – 'If I were you...'
involves understanding and empathy	does not involve empathy
respects others' rights to decide	makes the decisions

facilitating and leading groups

The idea of running a group development workshop can be a bit daunting, especially for managers who have had little or no experience in this area. But it is worth considering using this method because it can serve so many different purposes, for example:

- presenting new ideas or concepts;
- enabling people to learn from each other;
- building better team relationships;
- identifying and solving problems.

They are also valuable because within the safety of a workshop you can model (and you can get participants to practise) some of the behaviours that you want them to adopt outside in the workplace itself. The published agenda of the workshop may be 'Budgeting', 'Using the Telephone', or 'The Product and the Customer', but your behaviour and the methods that you use will help people to learn a sub-agenda of skills such as:

- communicating honestly and openly;
- working cooperatively;
- time management;
- expressing complex ideas;
- taking responsibility.

The very fact that you are holding the workshop is sending a powerful message to your team. It is telling them that you care about their opinions and that you believe it is important to involve them in plans for the future. What you do during the workshop is as important as what you say.

Here are some behaviours that you should make every effort to avoid:

- ignoring some individuals' contributions;

■ not making eye contact when you are talking;
■ embarrassing a team member to make a point;
■ talking for more than 50 per cent of the time;
■ aggressive or confrontational behaviour;
■ interrupting the session to take a phone call;
■ allowing one person to hog the discussion.

planning a workshop

Thorough planning will help to ensure that the event runs smoothly. In particular, think about what visual aids you could use, as these enable you to get your message across more effectively.

You need to plan the following:

■ *When you will hold the workshop and how long you want it to last:* unless you are a trained and experienced facilitator it is probably best to restrict the duration to a maximum of two hours.

■ *Where you will hold the workshop:* if possible you should use a quiet, spacious room away from the working environment where participants will be able to sit in comfort.

■ *What the aims of the workshop will be:* decide exactly what you want to achieve within the time that you have available.

■ *How you are going to achieve those aims:* if you do not plan this part carefully, you risk allowing the whole thing to degenerate into a pointless talking shop – or worse, a grumbling shop. Your task is to try to keep the workshop positive and focused on the future. If your overall goal is to empower people, you must ensure that you involve them actively by, for example:

– asking them questions;
– encouraging them to ask questions;

- giving them activities to work on in pairs or in small groups;
- getting them to present ideas to the full group;
- involving them in discussion.

In addition, you will need to prepare any pictures, posters, graphs or diagrams that you intend to use during the workshop. Make sure that a flipchart, flip pad and coloured pens will be available on the day.

your own development

We started off this section by pointing out that you are a learner too. Unfortunately, however, continuous professional development (CPD) is a low priority for many managers and therefore occurs in a fairly haphazard manner. We have little time or energy left to apply to our own development the same standards of quality that we specify for the opportunities we organise for other people.

But as a manager who seeks to empower others, it is vital that you overcome any resistance you may have to making your personal professional development a priority. You can't help others to learn unless you are involved in learning yourself.

1. In what ways have you developed over the past two years?

_____

_____

_____

_____

2. How has this development come about?

_____

_____

_____

_____

3. What unrealised potential do you consider you have?

_____

_____

_____

4. What constraints stop you realising this potential?

_____

_____

_____

5. What opportunities for development are open to you?

_____

_____

_____

You will probably have recognised that some development has taken place over the past months and that you have been able to take advantage of a variety of development opportunities. It is also likely that you have identified unfulfilled potential.

We have said that you should encourage the people who work with you to gain the maximum benefit from the development opportunities that occur naturally in the course of their work. In the same way you can train yourself to learn from the good and bad experiences that happen to you every day in your new role. You don't have to wait for a training manager to come along and identify your needs and put together a programme for you. You can instigate your own system of 'self-development'. This will ensure that you make the best use of your scarce time and resources and overcome any barriers that may stand between you and your personal goals and aspirations.

Successful self-developers tend to use some of the following to make their development less *ad hoc*. Tick the ones that you use at the moment.

Do you:

■ have a mentor? ☐
■ call on a network of people to support you? ☐
■ collect evidence of your development in a portfolio? ☐
■ plan your development in consultation with your line manager? ☐
■ review your plan and your achievements regularly? ☐
■ record your progress in a learning log? ☐

---

using a mentor

All learners can benefit in many important ways from having mentors. The role involves providing encouragement and support, helping to build self-confidence, challenging negative attitudes and offering constructive feedback. You should choose someone you can talk to easily, whom you can trust and who is willing to use his or her time on your behalf.

Your mentor could be:

■ a business colleague;

■ someone who has had recent experience of a programme of study;

■ a friend who understands what you are trying to achieve.

You can use a mentor in a number of ways and it is important that you think about the kind of support that you require. This checklist will help you decide what sort of relationship you want with your mentor.

Do you want your mentor to be:

1. a role model whom you can try to emulate? ☐
2. a dynamic person who can fill you with enthusiasm? ☐
3. a teacher who will help you to develop your skills? ☐
4. a powerful person who can open doors for you? ☐
5. a warm and caring listener? ☐
6. a tough taskmaster who sets high standards? ☐
7. a career counsellor? ☐
8. a person who is skilled in giving feedback? ☐
9. other? ☐

You can use this list as a starting point for identifying your expectations and requirements of a mentor. Not all potential mentors will be able to provide you with everything you want, but at least they will be able to tell you what they are prepared to offer. If you are open and honest with each other, you should be able to come up with a 'mentoring contract' that satisfies you both.

a support network

Although we have stressed your personal responsibility for your own development, this does not mean that you should isolate yourself from colleagues and friends who can offer moral support and practical help. Networking involves creating and using a wide-ranging list of people who can assist you in a variety of ways:

- your contacts, who can provide you with development opportunities;
- people with whom you can talk things over and who can help you to overcome problems;
- the network, which may be a source of feedback you have never tapped before.

Start to build up a list of contacts:

1. Inside your organisation

   _____
   _____
   _____
   _____

2. Outside your organisation

   _____
   _____
   _____

Once the list starts to build up, make a point of getting to know these people better. How can they help you? How can you help them? If you get used to asking for what you need, you will be surprised at the things others will be prepared to do to help.

building a development portfolio

A development portfolio is a continuous record of your achievements. It should contain evidence, not only of your qualifications and experience, but also of any courses or conferences that you have attended, books or journals that you have read, special projects that you have participated in and so on. In it you can show that you are aware of the considerable amount of learning that you achieve as you go about your day-to-day work, or that you derive from voluntary or leisure activities.

You can use a development portfolio for a number of purposes:

- ▓ to demonstrate your readiness for promotion;
- ▓ to gain academic recognition via credit accumulation (especially with regard to National Vocational Qualifications);
- ▓ for job interviews or assessment centres;
- ▓ as a basis for staff appraisal;
- ▓ as a development exercise in itself;
- ▓ to build your self-confidence.

The process of constructing a portfolio will require you to relate your achievements to your goals (or to national standards) and to present information clearly and concisely. It will also enable you to develop a sense of ownership of your past experiences and achievements.

You may already have a development portfolio, but if you have not, consider the reasons why you might decide to create one.

1. What would its purpose be?

_____

_____

_____

_____

2. Which items would you put in this development portfolio?

    _____

    _____

    _____

    _____

keeping a learning log

Self-developers have found that they gain more value out of the chaotic process of learning from everyday life if they discipline themselves to note down their experiences, their reflections, their ideas and their observations in a learning log.

There are many different ways of keeping a learning log, including:

- ▓ *Keeping a notebook:* the idea is that you keep a small notebook with you all day and jot down notes as they occur to you.
- ▓ *Keeping a personal journal:* this method involves regular logging in a more formal way. It implies a longer-term regular reflection on issues and events that seem important. To make sure that the reflection is systematised, headings are often used, for example:
  - experience (what happened);
  - reflection (what you think or feel about what happened);
  - learning (how what happened will affect what you do in future).
- ▓ *Analysing critical incidents:* here you make an entry only when you feel an experience was particularly important for your development. To be able to identify a critical incident you need to be aware of your goals and aspirations and your personal and professional priorities. You analyse an incident in two stages:

- what happened, who was there, how you felt and how these feeling influenced what you did;
- the nature of the incident or problem from the different points of view of the people involved;
- possible actions or solutions;
- how the learning can be converted to a plan of action for the future.

Learning logs are useful in development because they can identify problems and help you to recognise how to solve them. They can also help you to identify the skills which you need in order to address difficulties. As you assess yourself, honestly and privately, in the pages of a learning log, your self-awareness will also develop and your personal growth will be enhanced.

We have discussed mentors, support networks, development portfolios and learning logs in relation to your personal development. However, once you have tried them out for yourself and got a feel for ways in which they can benefit you, it is a good idea to recommend them to those people you are supporting.

In this chapter we have explored the theme of development and how it relates to empowerment. The next looks at some other ways in which you can encourage and motivate the people you want to empower.

accentuating the positive

You can't empower people unless they want to be empowered, and they won't give of their best unless they are motivated to do so. The experience of many high performing organisations seems to prove the old saying that 'Success breeds success'. The most important factor is that people should *feel* like winners – whether they are or not in reality does not seem to matter so much. This chapter is about gaining people's commitment and explores ways in which you can produce plenty of winners.

encouraging people to be more committed

This book is not the place to examine the psychology of motivation or motivation theories in great detail. You will find many texts on this subject on the shelves of your library or bookshop. Here I will simply explore a few practical points that may help you to generate commitment.

A few weeks ago my boss asked me to do some research into a new construction process and to write a report on it for the Board. I was excited about this opportunity to show what I could do, but in the event I found the job took me a lot longer than anticipated and was not as straightforward as I had hoped. To make matters worse, I was getting behind with my other work and this was causing me considerable stress. Halfway through the writing of the report, I showed the part that was finished to my colleague and asked him to tell me what he thought of it. He pointed out numerous errors and omissions – no doubt wanting to be helpful. However the result was that I had little heart to continue and the writing seemed to slow down even more than before.

I finally took the finished article to my boss feeling a bit like a schoolkid handing in an essay. His attitude could not have been more different – he was so encouraging. He said that the report was well thought out, that it was professionally written and that it contained some extremely interesting and important points. He did, however, point out one or two areas that could be improved before the report could be presented to the Board. I set about making these changes immediately, feeling 100 per cent more confident and enthusiastic than I had after my colleague had given her comments.

Anna, administration assistant in a property development company

get rid of the carrot and the stick

Classic motivation theory tells us that there are ultimately only two ways of making people do things: reward and punishment. The most basic motivation analogy conjures up a picture of a donkey standing in a field with a person trying to make it go through a gate. The idea is that the donkey will only move if you hit it with a stick or if you offer it a carrot.

One problem with this idea is that *you* can't actually motivate the donkey, it will only move if it feels sufficiently motivated – presumably inspired by fear of the stick or by the temptation of the carrot.

Motivation is an internal drive, not something you can impose on people from outside. All you can do is arrange things – build the structures, produce the systems, create an environment, develop relationships – so that people will feel motivated. If you have been able to implement some of the principles we have been discussing so far in this book, you will already be creating the kind of environment in which motivation can thrive. By giving people responsibility, you will make them feel that they 'own' the work processes in which they are involved. As owners, they will take a pride in their work and results will improve accordingly.

things that drive people

To achieve a motivating climate, however, you have to take into account the various factors that drive individuals. Think about your own experience for a moment. Make a list of two or three things that motivated you to achieve something that you found complex and difficult.

1. _____

2. _____

3. _____

It is sometimes said that people are driven by two sorts of motivating factors:

■ *Internal factors.* These include wanting to prove yourself, looking for a challenge, hoping for promotion, aiming for a personal goal or simply needing to keep busy.

■ *External factors.* Examples here could be feeling that a certain course of action will help with the job or improve the quality of life for you and your family.

In reality, most people are moved by a *combination* of internal and external factors, and this is valuable because the greater the motivation, the more effective people are in their work.

motivation through reward

Motivation can be further broken down in a number of ways. One of the most useful was suggested by Otto and Glaser in 1970. They analysed motivation in terms of the rewards that people can achieve through developing themselves at work.

Motivation	Reward
Achievement	Success
Anxiety	Avoidance of failure
Approval	Gaining the admiration and respect of others
Curiosity	Learning new things
Acquisitiveness	Money and other material benefits

Again, each of these motivating factors seldom acts in isolation. For example, someone could be motivated by achievement, the desire for approval and acquisitiveness at all the same time. The point is simply that if you find out about the most important motivating factors in individuals' lives you will be able to use this information to empower them:

■ If the motivating factor is predominantly *achievement*, you must ensure that the experience of empowerment is a successful one for the person or people involved. In this case it would be a mistake to allocate big tasks or an enormous amount of responsibility at first. Small, easily achievable steps which can frequently be rewarded would be better than ambitious aims that would take a long time to achieve.

■ If the motivating factor is predominantly *anxiety* you will need to help individuals to locate the source of their problem and to find ways of overcoming this. Excessive anxiety – a desire to avoid failure – constitutes a huge barrier to empowerment. In the early days, people in this group will need constant reassurance and a lot of positive feedback.

■ If the motivating factor is predominantly *approval*, individuals will need to know that you recognise their experience and their strengths. Once again they will require plenty of encouragement and praise for their achievements.

■ If the motivating factor is predominantly *curiosity*, you can build on this by providing tasks that will nurture their interests and their desire to find things out for themselves. People who are motivated by curiosity often enjoy interviewing customers, researching new developments or joining project teams.

■ If the motivating factor is predominantly *acquisitiveness*, you will need to stress how empowerment can lead to enhanced confidence and improved skills. This in turn will increase their chances of getting better jobs, higher salaries or other coveted material rewards.

positive reinforcement

In their book *In Search of Excellence*, Tom Peters and Alan Waterman point out that successful companies gain commitment from their people by making sure that they give them feedback or positive reinforcement on a regular, structured basis. In this discussion of the value of positive reinforcement Peters and Waterman draw on the work of the psychologist B F Skinner. The latter argued that we often depend far too much on criticism or punishment to bring about behavioural change and that, although such pressures do succeed in changing behaviour, this is often in an unpredictable and undesirable direction. Positive reinforcement, on the other hand, encourages appropriate behaviour and at the same time subtly 'nudges inappropriate behaviour off the agenda'.

In their book *In Search of Excellence*, Peters and Waterman give the example of an employee who is punished for 'not treating a customer well'. In this case the person concerned does not learn what to do in order to improve and he or she might well respond by trying to avoid customers altogether. The situation would be quite different if on the other hand someone tells the same person that a compliment has been received via a mystery shopper and that he or she handled a minor customer complaint 'in the best traditions of XYZ corporation'. The employee would now be more self-confident and keen to find other customers to treat well.

Consider for a moment how things are done in your organisation.

1. How often do you and others receive feedback on things you have done well?

_____

_____

_____

_____

2. To what extent does this feedback help you to know what is required of you in your work?

_____

_____

_____

_____

3. What proportion of this feedback is positive and what proportion is negative?

_____

_____

Peters and Waterman observed that most managers are still more likely to give and receive criticism rather than positive reinforcement. But the companies that produce the best results, the ones that succeed in empowering their workforce, are those that make an effort to provide positive feedback consistently and regularly.

giving feedback

Managers have always given their staff feedback. Basically it means telling people what you think of their behaviour, or informing them about the implications of their actions for other people or for the team, the department or the organisation as a whole. It is a specific and effective tool which empowers individuals in a number of important ways:

- ▓ It allows them to understand where their strengths are and the areas they may have to change.
- ▓ It lets them know about the progress they are making with regard to their personal goals and targets.
- ▓ It tells them that you are taking an interest in what they are doing.
- ▓ It underlines the importance of their work in the context of the wider organisation.
- ▓ It helps them to take a new perspective on their problems and concerns.

Feedback is empowering because it contributes to people's self-awareness. If it is competently given, it should also leave recipients with a choice – they do not have to act on the feedback unless they wish to do so.

positive feedback

Positive feedback is most useful if it is specific because people need to know exactly what it is they have done well. Saying, 'That is a good piece of work' may be nice for someone to hear, but it is not very helpful. You could instead try something like this:

> I think you made a very good presentation. You were very clear and to the point, with a good introduction and excellent punchy overheads. It was nice and short too – no-one had a chance to become bored or distracted.

Given the potential of feedback to increase motivation, it may be surprising to learn that many managers often either forget to give it or do not think that it is important. There is also an element of being too embarrassed to give praise because they think the recipient will be embarrassed.

But you only have to think back to your own experience if you need proof of the power of feedback. Do you remember the golden glow that you felt when people gave you specific positive comments on your behaviour or the things that you had produced? Do you also remember that tinge of bitterness when others fail to remark on the results of those hours you spent slaving over a piece of work?

negative feedback

Although this chapter stresses the need to remain positive, it is sometimes necessary to give negative feedback. This means telling people that their behaviour is in some way undesirable or that their work is not of the required standard. If you have ever had to give people this type of message, you will realise that negative feedback needs to be approached very carefully and sensitively. It is all too easy to demoralise someone by giving them negative feedback clumsily or angrily.

The trouble is that negative feedback is so often confused with criticism, and it is somehow much easier to criticise than to give feedback. The chart below summarises some of the differences between feedback and criticism.

Criticism:	Feedback:
▓ focuses on the person	▓ focuses on issues or problems
▓ harks back to the past	▓ looks to the future
▓ allocates blame	▓ looks for joint solutions to problems
▓ makes generalisations	▓ deals with particular episodes or situations
▓ says 'always' or 'never'	▓ makes specific comments
▓ starts from a position of hostility or aggression	▓ always uses positive, friendly approach

You will see some examples of criticism in the left-hand column below. One of them has been converted into feedback; use the guidelines above to help you convert the other two.

Criticism:	Feedback:
You're useless!	Mistakes like this one are preventing us from reaching our targets.
You don't seem to be interested in your work any more.	
Late again!	

Feedback is a vital ingredient of empowerment; it makes individuals more aware of themselves and brings them face to face with the consequences of their behaviour. But because we are so unused to the openness and honesty that is required during feedback, it can be very painful to receive negative comments. If you don't want to destroy a person's self-confidence, the feedback must be specific, positive and empowering.

You can give feedback in any situation – both in formal one-to-one meetings when you have a particular issue to deal with or informally, as and when the need arises. It is also useful to get others to give each other feedback and it is especially valuable to encourage the people you work with to give *you* feedback.

recognition

We have seen that empowering people means asking them to push themselves harder and to take on new responsibilities. It may involve encouraging them to accept a challenge, or even to make a journey into unknown territory. If they are to continue in this way and to encourage others to follow them, you must show that you appreciate their efforts and their achievements. Recognition, like constructive feedback, is another form of positive reinforcement.

A District Sales Manager was standing in the reception area of his office block, chatting to a colleague. 'It's terrible, I just can't trust the sales team to do anything', he was saying, 'I'd be better off just doing everything myself. Take this morning. When Dave went out I asked him to get me a sandwich on his way back in. I wouldn't mind betting that he lets me down.'

Just at that moment Dave came rushing in, breathless with excitement. 'I've done it!' he cried. 'I've just managed to close an order with Butterworth's for £20,000!'

'See what I mean?' sighed the Sales Manager. 'He forgot the sandwich!'

The way in which people are treated at work has a powerful effect on how they feel about themselves and on what they do. We all need to know that our work is noticed and appreciated, otherwise we feel excluded or demoralised. Research has shown that the more recognition managers provide, the more people are willing to extend themselves both for the organisation and for their own sense of self-fulfilment.

1. What schemes has your organisation introduced for recognising people's achievements?

    _____

    _____

    _____

    _____

2. How do you show others that you value what they do?

    _____

    _____

    _____

Because they have realised the vital importance of recognition in empowering and motivating people, many organisations have built formal recognition schemes into their systems and structures. Thus, in recent years we have seen the growth of, for example, long service awards, 'employee of the month' awards and productivity bonuses. However, it is equally important for empowering managers at all levels to devise their own recognition systems and to encourage a climate where everyone (not just managers) expresses their appreciation for colleagues' contributions.

The following list demonstrates the range of possible formal and informal recognition activities. It is more than likely that you already use several of these, maybe without even realising how powerful they are in empowering people:

- ■ *Taking a personal interest:* this makes others feel valued as individuals and not just 'cogs in a machine'. You may enquire about the health of the family or congratulate someone on sporting success, for example.
- ■ *Acknowledgements:* these are a written or verbal expression of appreciation for work well done. They can be directed at individuals or at entire teams or departments.
- ■ *Tangible rewards:* a whole gamut of rewards and prizes are frequently bestowed by organisations and individual managers to recognise valued achievements such as a challenging task accomplished well or a project completed within tight deadlines. Rewards may include a tray of cakes, a box of chocolates, theatre tickets or vouchers for meals or goods.
- ■ *Publicising success:* managers use noticeboards, newsletters or newspapers to make particular achievements public. Most people enjoy having their 'name in lights' in this way – but always check that you will not cause embarrassment.

Whichever forms of recognition you decide on, it is essential to take people's preferences into account. This story illustrates the dangers of assuming that everyone enjoys the same things as you and your colleagues.

The management team in a clothing factory decided on a recognition scheme where employees who had achieved high productivity were rewarded by being taken out to dinner at the company's expense. Each month a different manager would take the selected employee and his or her partner out to an expensive local restaurant. However, they were astonished to find that the majority of employees found the idea a daunting prospect rather than an exciting one.

'It would cost me a fortune to buy the right thing to wear', said one young woman. 'And I don't fancy the idea of trying to make conversation all evening with a boss I don't even know.'

By not thinking about the appropriateness of the reward, the whole point of the recognition scheme was lost. If it had continued, it would have been counterproductive because most employees did not want to win the award.

If you are in any doubt about the acceptability of recognition activities that you may be thinking of introducing, it is a good idea to ask for the views of the people who are to be on the receiving end of them. If you don't get this right you may end up (at best) by confusing or embarrassing people or (at worst) by offending or annoying them.

Find out what matters to the people who work with you.

1. Would they like the recognition to be public or private?

    _____

    _____

    _____

    _____

2. Would they like it to be formal or informal?

    _____

    _____

    _____

    _____

3. What form should the recognition take? (money? a gift? a badge? words of thanks? a combination?)

    _____

    _____

    _____

    _____

4. Should individuals be recognised or should the recognition be aimed at teams?

    _____

    _____

    _____

    _____

If the theory and practice of recognition is new for you, it is vital to tell individuals and teams why you are now giving them recognition. You should also be prepared to admit that you may have missed valuable opportunities to do this in the past.

learning to love conflict

> Conflict in the sense of contrast of ideas is not undesirable; only through expression of difference can good problem-solving take place. Contrast can lead to clarification, progress or seeing a way forward.
> *Effective Teambuilding by John Adair*

Although this chapter emphasises the importance of taking a positive attitude, this does not mean that negative feelings should be buried and that conflict should be avoided. There are two reasons for this:

1. Conflict can allow innovative ideas to be generated and discussed.

2. Conflicts that remain unexpressed and unresolved are almost certain to cause problems later on.

There must be a firm foundation of openness and trust, however, before a work group can make constructive use of differences of point of view. If people are honest, disagreements can be aired and more easily resolved. If people feel able to state their views without worrying that they may be laughed at or victimised, they are on the way to becoming truly empowered. If, however, there is not enough trust in the team for members to be able to express their opinions openly, a great deal of energy may be wasted and potentially valuable ideas will be lost.

Consider the following questions in relation to the people you manage:

1. Does each person express his or her views openly?
2. Do people listen to each others' opinions – and value them?
3. Are people able to put forward differences of opinion without this becoming a slanging match?
4. Will people express the same views to you that they share with other members of the group?

Achieving openness and trust with the people you work with should allow you to profit from the creative ideas that often flow from constructive disagreements.

Empowering managers do not necessarily avoid conflicts between the people they work with. Instead they acknowledge that they happen and make use of them – harnessing the enthusiasm and ideas that are produced to improve the quality of people's work. True empowerment actually *depends* on healthy and constructive conflict.

This chapter has explored some of the ways in which you can empower people by gaining their commitment: finding out what motivates them, making them feel like winners and demonstrating that you value and appreciate their efforts and their achievements. The final chapter turns to examine some practical ways in which you can start to empower people today.

act now!

Empowering people may sometimes feel like pushing a boulder up a steep hill – at least in the early days. But if you know what you are aiming to achieve and you plan your strategy well – and most of all if you believe in the value of what you are doing – your efforts will ultimately be rewarded.

This final chapter includes a round up of a few practical ideas that you can put into practice straight away. It starts with a discussion of ways in which you can influence people in your organisation so that they will support you in your empowering activities. It finishes with an action plan that will help you to make empowerment a way of life.

influencing

In your role as an empowering manager you will need to influence a variety of people: your colleagues, the people who are responsible to you, your line manager, maybe even the Board of Directors or their equivalent if you are in the public sector or a voluntary organisation. Your influence can help to change people's attitudes or their behaviour patterns. It will be difficult to empower others or to introduce empowering systems within your organisation if you are unable to influence people positively.

The extent to which you are successful in influencing will depend on your understanding of:

■ when to influence;
■ who to influence;
■ which approach to take in the circumstances;
■ the skills that you need to apply in a particular situation.

when your influence is required

Some of the situations in which you will need to influence others are:

■ *When you want to gain their commitment:* here you will be getting others to pay attention to your ideas, to appreciate the benefits of empowerment and to gain their support for the process.
■ *When you want to get people involved:* here you will be persuading others to accept the idea of empowerment and to become involved in an appropriate capacity.
■ *When you want to make empowerment a way of life:* here you must ensure that people will not opt out as soon as their initial enthusiasm has subsided. It will involve you and others in providing plenty of support and encouragement until empowerment really has become embedded in the organisation's culture.

selecting the right strategy

There are two basic ways of influencing people:

1. the *push* strategy; and
2. the *pull* strategy.

pushing

Pushing is directive (or may even be authoritarian), and so has to be used sensitively and sparingly. It is only likely to be successful if the people you are pushing are very inexperienced or have a low level of self-confidence. Even then you must avoid patronising them, overwhelming them or sparking off a rebellion. It is vital that you take time to discuss your strategy fully and explore any problems or worries with the people concerned.

This case study illustrates how a team leader introduced an empowerment initiative using the push strategy.

Nasreen is catering manager in a staff canteen in central Birmingham. Her company 'Excel Catering' holds the catering contracts in a number of factories and commercial premises all over the Midlands, Wales and the South West of England. But competition for contracts is tough and Excel is being squeezed hard by its clients on both quality and price.

She has been advised by her area manager that the only way to meet current targets is to change the roles of the kitchen staff so that they are no longer just operatives carrying out her instructions. But how to do this? The older ones have been brought up to think of themselves as 'employees', and are not used to working on their own initiative. Many of the younger ones are too timid to imagine that anything they have to say might be of value.

Nasreen decided that her only option was to start by pushing forward a plan for empowering a small number of the staff. She asked for volunteers to join a group that would work with her to plan how to achieve the targets that had been set. She started the meeting off by setting the scene, identifying the problems that confronted them and making her proposal for forming this group into a problem-solving team. She then invited reactions and questions and dealt with objections as positively and persuasively as possible. Then she checked that she had understood what the group had been saying to her and summarised their discussions.

> Having made sure that those present still wanted to be involved, she planned with them who would do what and by when.

Note that Nasreen's strategy involves identifying exactly what she wants to achieve and then using her own power to persuade others to become involved. She is gambling on the fact that the group will eventually experience the benefits of becoming empowered, so that she will no longer have to be so directive in her approach.

pulling

This strategy involves a group of people in deciding what to do, rather than having one person decide on behalf of the others. It is a process that can be more effective and more appropriate in gaining others' commitment, although it may also be more time-consuming. Having agreed what the problem is, you can then work with the individual or the group to find a solution before finally coming to a mutual agreement about what is to be done, by whom and by when.

Pulling is more directly empowering than pushing because it draws on other people's ideas, gains their commitment and develops trust. The outcome may be harder for you to accept because others will not always agree with your views. However, it is vital that you work out what the best outcome is for everyone concerned – especially those who will eventually have to live and work with the plans that you decide on.

It is often appropriate to push in the early stages – especially if, as we have seen, others lack experience and are afraid of making mistakes. The well-judged push is often what is needed to break an impasse and get empowerment going.

Are you predominantly a pusher or a puller?

Which of the following tactics do you use to persuade others to do things?

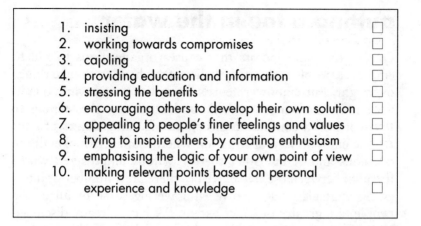

1. insisting ☐
2. working towards compromises ☐
3. cajoling ☐
4. providing education and information ☐
5. stressing the benefits ☐
6. encouraging others to develop their own solution ☐
7. appealing to people's finer feelings and values ☐
8. trying to inspire others by creating enthusiasm ☐
9. emphasising the logic of your own point of view ☐
10. making relevant points based on personal experience and knowledge ☐

You may find that you use a combination of push strategies (which are those with the odd numbers) and pull strategies (the even-numbered ones), but that, like most people, you have a preference for one or the other approach. It is important to recognise your strengths but you must also ensure that you are competent in both types, because you will need them when you are empowering others.

This list shows how you might push and pull when you are introducing empowerment into your organisation, department or team:

Push	for getting people to listen
Pull	for gaining their commitment
Push	for setting goals and targets
Pull	for getting people involved
Push	for action planning
Pull	for sustaining interest and commitment

It's a bit like a rowing boat – you will make progress much faster if you alternate these opposing forces. You will find it valuable to identify the influencing skills that you may need to develop, and how you can use these to empower people.

putting a toe in the water

One of the main factors that causes organisations to fail to empower people is that they believe they have to change things overnight. But empowerment is not a black and white condition; it is much more realistic and much less threatening to think of it as a continuum incorporating many shades of grey. At one end you have a situation where managers make all the decisions and at the other there is a fully empowered workforce. In between the two extremes there are a number of interesting strategies that involve empowering some or all of the people to a greater or lesser extent. We have already discussed some of these, and others are explored later in this chapter. They include:

- introducing systems for sharing information;
- using employee suggestion schemes;
- encouraging people to take responsibility for their own development;
- forming quality circles/focus groups;
- involving people in decision making and problem solving;
- developing teamwork.

What this means is that you don't have to introduce empowerment throughout the organisation before you have tried it out in one or two areas and ironed out some of the problems. Depending on the circumstances you could:

- target one department or section of the organisation as a 'pilot' for everyone else;
- select appropriate people as empowerment 'champions' who can develop themselves and go on to support others;
- use a particular problem or project as a vehicle for developing the concept and practice of empowerment.

Whatever you decide to do, you must be open about it with the whole workforce. People will start to become nervous and suspicious if they see that others are selected for special initiatives or projects that they know nothing about. You must also guard against empowerment projects becoming elitist – make it clear that there will be opportunities for everyone when and if they want them.

Once you have tried out empowering strategies with a few groups and individuals it will be much easier to plan how to develop this approach more widely throughout the organisation.

developing teamwork

Teamworking is a key strategy both for empowering people and for improving organisational performance. Team members seem to derive considerable satisfaction from working in cooperation with others and teams are both more productive and more efficient than individuals working on their own.

---

case study: Yardley

Louise and her team on the lipstick line at Yardley used to have a hard job lifting heavy boxes of containers onto the automatic lipstick filling machine known as 'Alf'. They decided that the solution lay either in bringing the lipstick containers to the factory in smaller boxes or fitting a conveyor belt to do the lifting for them. The second option proved to be the cheaper and the company has now agreed to buy a small conveyor...

When teams were asked to look at ways of cutting down on waste... the mascara and eyeliner team came up with an idea that has saved around £10,000 within a year.

'Each team consists of about 11 people and for 11 people to

save that much money is quite a lot,' says the manager of the cosmetics unit. 'What we have done is tell the team members that they are the experts and they should tell us what they need to run their lines efficiently. My role is to encourage them, to coach them and to get them to use their own initiative.'

Teamworking started in an almost *ad hoc* way, which meant that it did not require any form of training or management involvement. All it needed was to get internal 'customers' and 'suppliers' to talk to each other. Initially managers were not keen to describe what was happening as total quality, or teamworking or empowerment, but they said simply 'this is common sense'.

Source: 'More than just a cosmetic change', an article in *People Management* by Anat Arkin, 20 April 1995.

The best teams are known as 'high-performing teams', 'self-managing teams' or sometimes 'superteams'. Because such teams are so rare and so productive, they are worth their weight in gold. These are some of the qualities that differentiate successful teams from ordinary teams:

- They have a clear sense of a shared purpose.
- They are inventive in their efforts to remove the obstacles that prevent them from achieving their aims.
- They have high expectations of themselves and others.
- The members communicate effectively both with each other and with those outside the team.
- They are committed to the success of their parent organisation.
- They expect their leader to support them and to fight for adequate resources so that they can achieve their purpose.
- They are constantly looking for ways to do things better.

Think of a team of which you are a leader or a member. Which of the above qualities does it possess?

_____

_____

_____

_____

Which ones does it need to develop?

_____

_____

_____

The Yardley case study tells us a lot about the benefits of the team approach for organisations, but it has been shown that this approach is also highly beneficial for team members. The teamwork process gets results because:

■ It provides people with an opportunity to have their abilities appreciated by others.
■ Members can learn from working closely with others.
■ People have the chance to achieve something they could not do on their own.
■ Teamwork is often an enjoyable and rewarding experience.

Those companies that have successfully introduced teamworking are probably further down the road to empowering their people than many others that are using alternative strategies.

involving people in decision making

When people are involved in making a good decision you gain in two ways:

1. The outcome of the successful decision.
2. The increased confidence, motivation and commitment of those involved. This will be likely to produce further successful decision making.

Traditionally, managers or leaders have assumed the authority to take decisions alone and to pass them down the line for implementation. But empowering organisations try to ensure that key decisions are made by appropriate work groups or management teams. Decisions made by the wrong people at the wrong time can have disastrous implications when they are implemented.

There are many techniques and processes that can help you and your team to make decisions and solve problems. In fact there are no 'right' or 'wrong' ways of making decisions – only those that do or do not succeed in keeping people motivated and empowered. The methods you adopt must suit the needs of the task, of the team and of its members.

Decision making processes can be put into two broad categories:

1. logical analysis
2. creative or lateral processes.

Managers often use a combination of both approaches to help with a particular decision.

logical analysis

This is a linear approach to decision making. It is useful when you have plenty of information and a large group of people who can get involved. One of the better known methods in this category is **DECIDE**.

These are the steps:

Define carefully what the issue actually is.

Examine all the facts relating to the issue; what are the circumstances, why is it important, who else is involved etc.

Consider the options.

Involve other people to generate alternative ideas and ways of looking at the problem.

Decide what to do and then act on your decision.

Evaluate the results of the decision. How might you improve the process next time?

creative processes

Creative, or 'lateral', techniques are ways of generating innovative solutions to tricky problems. They help you to avoid the blind alleys that can sometimes be the end results of logical analysis. One of the most commonly used methods in this category is brainstorming.

This activity harnesses the energy of a group to create ideas, make decisions or solve problems. Members of the group are asked to suggest ideas relating to the problem or situation, and to be as free as possible in their thinking. One of the group (often the team leader or manager) writes down the suggestions as they are produced so that everyone can see what has gone before and associations and links are allowed to flow freely.

The rules of brainstorming are:

1. Write down exactly what people say.
2. Do not stop to discuss or evaluate suggestions during the brainstorm, as this interrupts the free flow of ideas.
3. The time to categorise and evaluate all the suggestions is when the brainstorm is complete. At this point the group draws up a shortlist of the most feasible ideas.
4. Sift through the suggestions, perhaps discarding the ones which are not feasible. Through a process of discussion and refining, finally decide which one to adopt and put into practice.

The technique should enable the group to come up with more innovative ideas than would have been generated by individuals working alone. When groups use creative techniques it is valuable because they feel ownership of the ideas they come up with.

quality circles

A quality circle is a group of four to twelve people, usually coming from the same work area, who meet on a regular basis to discuss, analyse and solve their work-related problems. A circle presents its solutions to management and is frequently involved in implementing and monitoring them. The original development of quality circles occurred in Japan, but the idea has now spread throughout the world.

> When quality circles were introduced in Gregg Bakeries Ltd, thirty per cent of the workforce volunteered to become members. The different groups achieved many improvements during their first ten years. For example:
>
> ■ they introduced an improved design of dolly wheel for transporting and storing savoury products;

- they set up a more effective cleaning programme;
- they set up a routine procedure for preventing wet floors during production hours;
- they investigated reasons for the high occurrence of back-related injuries and proposed correct lifting procedures for briefing to all staff;
- they also set up new cleaning rotas, improved bread bag sizes, introduced a cleaning and maintenance system for all bakery racks and suggested methods for saving ingredients.

The QC idea has been taken up enthusiastically by staff because it encourages total staff involvement regardless of their status or position. The scheme has also helped in breaking down the barriers between workers and management.

Source: *Quality Circles*, published by the Department of Trade and Industry

The experience of organisations like Greggs has shown that the following factors are important to the success of a QC programme:

- Top management must support the idea.
- Members must participate voluntarily.
- Operational managers must give their support and participate actively.
- Training must be provided for facilitators, leaders and members.
- Those in the circle must come from a shared work background.
- Circles must be solution orientated.
- Solutions must be implemented once they have been accepted.
- The achievements of quality circles must be publicly recognised.

empowerment as a way of life

Both this and previous chapters contain various ideas for making empowerment happen for people you work with. But there is a danger that the concept will remain an impossible dream unless you plan carefully where you want to go and how you will get there. If you set off on a journey without clear goals and direction, you will never arrive at the desired destination. Decide what you want to achieve and how you want to achieve these things, give yourself some clear targets and deadlines and decide who can help you. Make effective use of a mentor and your support network as discussed in Chapter 4.

You will also find it useful to monitor the results of your chosen strategy. This will involve you in identifying the 'success criteria' to look for. Once these factors start to emerge, you will know that your strategy is reaping rewards. In the short term you may look for improvements such as:

■ a happier team;
■ a more motivated team;
■ a more relaxed atmosphere;
■ barriers between different groups breaking down;
■ better internal communications.

In the long term you may look for effects such as:

■ improved productivity;
■ greater efficiency;
■ fewer customer complaints;
■ lower staff turnover;
■ reduced absenteeism.

involving people in evaluation

Evaluation is how you find out the extent to which the agreed targets of empowerment activities have been achieved. It is important for several reasons:

- ▓ It allows people to identify how far their activities have been effective.
- ▓ People can get feedback on how well they have done and on where they need to improve.
- ▓ The evaluation of one activity can give people an idea of what to do next.

Evaluation is usually the starting point for the next cycle of finding new ways to empower people.

You will need to ask people to look at both the outcomes of the task or project and the actual experience itself when you are reviewing their activities.

Consider a recent project or activity and review its outcomes and the experience with the group or person involved. You can use these questions to help you review:

1. What were the targets of the project?
2. Were these targets achieved?
3. In what ways has the project helped to improve the performance of the team/individual?
4. How has it contributed to organisational or team goals?
5. How have our customers benefited?
6. What unexpected spin-offs arose as a result of the project?
7. Was this the best approach to use?
8. How could it have been improved?
9. Were there enough resources?
10. What else was needed?

11. Was the support given appropriate and was there enough of it?
12. Were the resources used adequate? What else was needed?

Evaluation will enable you and others to gather a lot of useful information. You will find out which kind of approaches work well and which are not quite so valuable. You will also learn about the types of support needed by different people.

If the evaluation highlights some real successes, don't be afraid to publicise these and to celebrate them with those who have been involved. Remember that celebrating the things people have done well is essential if you want to maintain your team's enthusiasm for becoming more independent and more empowered. All too often in our British culture success goes unremarked, while failures are chewed over at length.

Your own reward for your hard work will be, at the very least, increased job satisfaction at seeing people beginning to achieve their full potential. More than that you can expect to know yourself better, find where your power lies and improve your promotion prospects!

> The wise leader is not collecting a string of successes. The leader is helping others to find their own success. There is plenty to go around. Sharing success with others is very successful.
>
> *The Tao of Leadership by John Heider*

Reading this book is just one step on the journey to empowering other people; now it is crucial to set your goals, make your plans, find your support and take action.

summary

In this book I have set out to explore with you:

- what empowerment is and how it can benefit organisations and individuals;
- the type of culture in which empowerment will flourish;
- the nature of empowering relationships;
- how you can empower people by simply communicating with them;
- the role of development in empowering people;
- the importance of developing yourself;
- how to gain people's commitment;
- some of the practical things you can do to empower people.

However enthusiastic you are to become an empowering manager, don't forget that you will have a greater chance of success if you gain the support of other managers and the organisation as a whole. Take care to involve key people from the beginning and use your influencing skills to gain their commitment and support.

references and further reading

Adair, John (1986) *Effective Teambuilding*, Pan Books, London.

Berne, Eric (1961) *Transactional Analysis in Psychotherapy*, Evergreen.

Blanchard, Kenneth H. (1999) *The 3 Keys to Empowerment*, Berrett-Koehler.

Clemmer, Jim and McNeil, Art (1989) *Leadership Skills for Every Manager*, Piatkus, London.

Handy, Charles (1995) *The Empty Raincoat*, Arrow Business Books.

Heider, John (1993) *The Tao of Leadership*, Gower Publishing, Aldershot.

Honey, Peter and Mumford, Alan (1988) *The Manual of Learning Styles*, Peter Honey.

Johnson, Mike (1995) *Managing in the Next Millennium*, Butterworth–Heinemann, Oxford.

McGregory, Douglas (1987) *The Human Side of Enterprise*, Penguin Books, Harmondsworth.

Peters, Tom (1987) *Thriving on Chaos*, Pan Books, London.

Peters, Thomas and Waterman, Robert (1982) *In Search of Excellence*, Harper and Row, New York.

Shaw, George Bernard (1990) *Pygmalion*, Penguin Books, Harmondsworth.

Visit Kogan Page on-line

Comprehensive information on
Kogan Page titles

Features include

- complete catalogue listings,
  including book reviews and
  descriptions

- on-line discounts on a variety
  of titles

- special monthly promotions

- information and discounts on
  NEW titles and BESTSELLING titles

- a secure shopping basket facility
  for on-line ordering

- infoZones, with links and
  information on specific areas of
  interest

PLUS everything you need to know
about KOGAN PAGE

http://www.kogan-page.co.uk